I WANT TO COMPLAIN!
: An alternative guide to customer service

(Helping to put the 'fun' into refund and the 'jest' into goodwill gesture)

© 2011 Peter Nuttall
ISBN : 978-1467906098

www.peternuttall.net

Contents

Preface

After working in the complaints departments for a multi-national retailer and a nationwide public service organisation for over eight years, I've dealt with my fair share of customer complaints and queries. It was one thing dealing with a complaint about a broken down fridge and hundreds of pounds worth of spoiled food but quite another to deal with a client who had received too many screws for his bookcase and then rang back seven times an hour until I agreed to arrange for a sales person from a local store to go to his house and collect them.

I grew weary to the point of rolling my eyes, no matter how valid a customer complaint was, no matter how well constructed it was, no matter how concise or only containing relevant facts it was and found myself only taking interest in the letters of complaint that were short or funny. If I received a letter that was ten pages long, detailing everything the customer had done from waking up, putting their slippers on and having a shave, I would skip to the last paragraph because that would invariably be where the customer would make their demands, be it a new door handle or compensation. I wholeheartedly agree with the consumer advice professionals who say your letters of complaint should be succinct and only contain relevant facts but the vast majority of complaints handlers have been in the job for far too long and most believe they should really be somewhere else, doing something else. One consumer body I spoke to said you should complement the company you're complaining to, i.e. 'I have bought your crumpets for years and never had an issue'. No one other than the person who made the crumpets cares whether you eat and enjoy them or use the crumpets as Frisbees.

However, my experience of handling complaints certainly helped when I had to write my own letter of complaint about a parking fine. I avoided all the things that annoyed me about other people's complaint letters and made it as light-hearted as possible without sounding condescending. I had my parking ticket rescinded with a cheeky reply. I tried the same thing with *Virgin Media* and *Asda*; again, prompt action, apologies and refunds were forthcoming.

Instead of looking at failures of service as a reason to sound off at someone, I took it as an opportunity to be creative, lighten the complaint handler's day and put myself at the front of the queue for service recovery. After writing numerous letters and receiving favourable outcomes to my gripes, I thought it a good idea to share my letters with consumers such as yourself to use as a template the next time the company you have given the money you spent hours of your life working for, gives you meagre service in return.

As I eventually ran out of issues that directly affected me, I started to write complaint letters for friends and eventually, people who visited my website, *www.iwanttocomplain.net;* Maybe there is a letter somewhere in this book which sums up exactly how you feel – if so, please feel free to use it in your attempt to redress whatever injustice you have experienced. I do think however, that it is important not only for the person responsible for the level of customer service you receive to empathise with you, but also you with them. Being a customer service advisor is a thankless job. Even when you do get thanks, it does nothing to erase the memory of the customer yelling expletives for half an hour down the phone at you. I can only conclude that it is my experience in the industry which helped me to gain favourable outcomes to my complaints. I have therefore attempted to provide an insight for you the consumer, into the world of the complaints handler, to arm you fully in the fight against poor customer service and consumer justice.

What is it to complain?

In this book I will approach the art of complaining from a number of different angles. I will look at it from the perspective of those who handle the complaints; hopefully those of you who make complaints in the future can understand the world of someone who has to listen to people complaining to them all day. I will take a look into a day in the life of a call centre agent and what exactly goes on behind the microphone. I will also look at the complaint procedure from the point of view of the customer, and hopefully open the minds of those who have lost the sense of fun that can come with such a job. There are many practical consumer advice books and websites out there but none really find out who the people we're dealing with are, what they're thinking and how to best communicate with them. In the second section of the book there are genuine letters of complaint I have written and sent over the last few years including their replies. With these letters, I hope to prove my hypothesis that light-hearted letters get more favourable results than 'shouty' ones.

Everyone is somebody's customer. Whether you're buying a packet of mints from your local corner shop or purchasing your third helicopter from *Copters and Things Ltd.*, I can think of no reason why the person buying the mints should expect an inferior level of service to the person buying the AH-64 Apache. It's perhaps a myth that the British are prone to 'let things slide' in a situation where the service is dire, rather than cause a scene. This is certainly truer in restaurants as it's probably not a good idea to send food back to the kitchen for any reason as the replacement dish's contents may be a little more 'phlegmy' than its predecessor.

You can categorise complainers into one of the following groups :

The Trivial complainer

Issues complaints such as 'my car has run out of petrol' and 'an ice cream man parks outside your store in Camden and the noise really upsets my dog'. Whether these complaints are genuine or not, they are generally directed at someone who has no responsibility for it. Why would you complain to Vauxhall if the sun was too bright while you were driving to work this morning?

Serial complainers

The serial complainer will ring, send a letter, an e-mail, a fax and a carrier pigeon to get their message across. They will never give up, no matter how far in the wrong they are, demanding compensation for the fact their curtains haven't been delivered for two days and the sunshine has woken them up too early.

Professional complainers

They know who to write to, what to write and how to get straight to the top. They are generally the people that the complaints manager will pay compensation to 'get rid of'. They generally write things in block capital letters.

The Pedant

This complainer will always start their letter or conversation with something similar to "I first purchased my car on a slightly overcast 12th January 2011 from a sales man called Jeff who had a small mole on his left cheek". They will then go on to describe every detail of the transaction and, after reaching page 4 of the complaint letter, you realise that they have only just reached the point where their car first started making a 'funny noise'. They will then proceed to explain this funny noise in detailed wording such as 'whizzing', 'burbling' and 'buzzing'. None of these words really help you to diagnose the problem as, you are not a mechanic. When you speak to this customer on the telephone, they will tell you that you are incompetent and you shouldn't be working in customer services if you can't diagnose their car's fault over the phone.

The Liar

This complainer will tell both white and wild lies about their 'customer journey' thus far. They will insist that they weren't given any terms and conditions to sign, nor were they advised that their delivery could be between the hours of 8am and 6pm. They will also tell you that they've been on hold to the call centre for an hour, when in reality, they got straight through, just to exaggerate what they describe as 'a living nightmare from which they feel they may never awaken'. It turns out later that even though they were told by three separate people when the delivery would be made, they 'popped to the shop' and were out when the driver turned up. They will never admit that it was their fault.

The Indifferent

The ones who write in then forget that they've written or if they don't get a reply, they're not too fussed. They generally say things like "the wallpaper in your store clashed with your carpets" or "the salesman had a bushy moustache. I was scared of him."

The type of letters I used to enjoy reading in my time as a complaints handler were the light-hearted ones, the ones that made me laugh and outlined the complaint without making me treat it as 'another complaint letter'. The light hearted letters and e-mails tended to get the more favourable responses. Letters that contain phrases like "I'm going to tell my solicitor" and "If you don't replace my sink, you'll be sorry", were always pushed to the back of the queue and handled with not a little apathy. If you sit at a desk listening to customers complain for eight hours a day, the last thing you want is another letter written in red pen, underlined with every other sentence punctuated with eight exclamation marks.

Why are you complaining?

You might have a genuine complaint brought on by a rude member of staff, inferior goods or a late delivery. You might just be frustrated with a company's policy and procedure. You might just want some free stuff. There are several ways to lodge a complaint with a company.

Letter

Whenever you speak to consumer advice bodies like Consumer Direct, Trading Standards or Citizens Advice Bureaux, they advise you to put your complaint in writing. This is good advice, but in my experience your letter will end up with one of the following responses :

"Thank you for raising this issue, it will be handled internally – sorry for any inconvenience caused." In other words, they haven't read it, sent out a standard letter and don't propose to do anything at all about it.

It will be laughed at because you wrote something like "The cooker overheated and melted my knob" – and then photocopied, sent round the office and then left on the photocopier. The next person to use the copier will then think this is finished with and dispose of it in the shredder.

It gets allocated to a customer service agent, not the managing director to whom you wrote. They ring you with empty and shallow apologies and then call you names to their colleagues while holding the mute button on their phone. They call you more names when they hang up, reciting the whole conversation, inserting false accounts of how you swore at them and called them names, even though you didn't.

They find the letter amusing, which is a breath of fresh air to a complaints handler. They look forward to speaking to you and helping you.

There are certain things you'd think would make the customer service department take your letter more seriously but in reality, only make the reader roll their eyes, sigh and put it on the bottom of the pile of letters they have to deal with that day :

- <u>Underlining words</u>
- Putting more than one exclamation mark at the end of sentences!!!
- Using a red pen for certain words
- Writing some words twice as big as others
- WRITING IN CAPITALS
- Threatening things that you couldn't possibly achieve, such as closing their company down because they delivered your shirt a day late
- Inappropriate and badly placed swear bloody words
- Self-pity – what disease your mother-in-law has, how many hours a week you have to work and how red your ear went while holding on the customer service line which is never answered etc…
- Being aggressive (which only scares temporary staff and school leavers – and they don't generally deal with complaint letters).
- <u>UNDERLINING WORDS</u>, USING RED PEN, WRITING SOME WORDS TWICE AS BIG AS OTHERS WITH BADLY BLOODY PLACED SWEAR WORDS BLOODY IN CAPITALS **AND** WITH MORE THAN ONE EXCLAMATION MARK AT THE END OF SENTENCES **IN BOLD**!!!

E-Mail

Large companies will have a team of 3 or 4 people who sit and wait for
e-mail enquiries and complaints to arrive. Bear in mind that they don't
have to endure call after call from shouting customers and are
therefore much more helpful with your complaints as they are
generally in a better mood than those on the phones. Companies who
trade through their websites however very rarely have incoming
telephone lines – and as such, their E-mail customer service agents
have the same mind-set of those who are shouted at by customers all
day. The e-mails will end up with one of the following responses :

- Being forwarded around the office because you complained
  quite passionately about the sign outside the shop blowing to a
  forty-five degree angle, hitting you in the arm and damaging
  your favourite Argyle cardigan.

- Being accidentally deleted by a trainee who has only just found
  out what a computer is.

- Being filed in the recycle basket.

- A response so luke-warm you could bath your new born twins
  in it.

Telephone

Most large companies have call centres. Most call centres have their
fair share of people who have just left school or are working there part
time between being a mother or a student. In all cases, the people you
speak to have been sitting in the same seat, being yelled at eight hours
a day, five days a week for as long as they can remember. They all
know there is more to life and it is this thought that prevents them from
focusing on their job, deciding instead to think about which specialist
jobs newspaper they are going to buy at lunchtime. In short, they hate
their job and they hate customers.

Things happening while you are yelling at a customer service agent :

- They are imagining you being chased by a large hungry dog.

- They are on the internet looking at *www.bored.com* and not listening to a word you are saying.

- They are e-mailing the person sitting next to them about where they're meeting that night to get drunk and forget all about where they work.

- They are staring at the clock, counting the seconds down to their next break.

- They are mouthing along sarcastically to your complaints and making a funny face.

- They are waiting for an opportunity to put you on hold so they can concentrate on getting the ball in the hole on a game they found on *www.bored.com* – they come back to you after four *Vivaldi* filled minutes to tell you they can't do anything.

- They are attempting to eat an entire bag of crisps without you stopping mid-scream to ask what that 'funny crunchy noise' is.

Escalation

This is the key. If you call, ask for the Director of Corporate Affairs; don't ask for the Managing Director or the Chief Executive as they will have a team of agents set up to take calls on their behalf. Be warned, these agents are seasoned; they have been on every team in the call centre and are now versed in the art of saying "No", "I can't" and "You will have to put it in writing". It is much easier to speak to a Marketing Director or the Retail Director, and they won't realise you are actually calling to complain.

You could also mention you have spoken to a local TV company for their show "Rouge Retailers" (make it up if you have to) and they will then ensure that you are called back, given compensation and sent flowers.

3rd Party advice

Free 3rd Party advice is available in a number of places. They're handy if you want to know about legislation, sale of goods and services act or your statutory rights. If you want action though, you're going to have to contact a solicitor which can be expensive and you actually have to have a case to present and not just a salesperson who looked at you funny.

A day in the life of a call centre agent

08:00 - I rolled out of bed after getting four hours of sleep, having lain awake for five hours last night dreading going into work today.

08:45- I took a slow dawdle down the hill to work, looking only at my shoes, beaten as I am by only ever experiencing the aggressive, irritable and irascible side of human nature day after day.

09:01 - I got shouted at by a team leader who is younger than me for logging into my telephone ten seconds late. She told me that I am paid from nine o'clock, not ten seconds past.

09:03 - I took my first call of the day which was from someone who said their delivery was late. I explained that it could be anytime from eight until twelve.

09:07 - I took my second call of the day from the same customer, still asking where their delivery was as it hadn't turned up yet.

09:09 - I typed rude words into the customer database to see if there were any customers with funny names. My team leader caught me chuckling and asked if I was alright – not in the caring sense, in the threatening 'take a call or you'll be on a disciplinary' sense.

09:10 - I was subjected to my colleague Stephen's daily rant about how he is only working in a call centre until something better comes along. He has a degree in Social Science. I then had to listen to Sophie who explained that she is here because she failed miserably at school and the criteria for the job was (a) must be breathing (b) must have a vague grasp of the English language (c) must be able to type things into computers (d) ability to wear a headset. I watched as neither of them showed any enthusiasm for the job they're being paid minimum wage to do then Sophie hung up on another customer mid-complaint.

09:14 - I got the customer that Sophie hung up on and he was even angrier than before. I squinted at Sophie to show my displeasure but she remained oblivious to this and hung up on another customer.

09:43 - I got shouted at again by my team leader because I should be taking ten calls an hour. I try to explain that it isn't possible because everyone in the entire building had only taken ten calls between them so far today. I was told to stop being cheeky or I'd be on a disciplinary. I felt depressed.

10:01 - I spoke to my first angry customer of the day and after hearing him shout for six minutes, seemingly without breathing, I had to conform to the 'call quality' rules and ask him if there was anything else I could help him with. He then shouted at me for the next ten minutes, seemingly without breathing. I put him on mute, went on the internet and looked up 'melancholy' on *Wikipedia*. Once he'd stopped shouting, I again had to conform to the 'call quality' rules and ask him if he'd considered changing his home insurance provider. He shouted at me for a third time, for another ten minutes.

10:40 - The customer finally hung up – well, his mobile battery ran out. I missed my break so I wasn't allowed to take it. I pressed the 'not ready' button on my phone and folded my arms petulantly until my team leader asked why I hadn't taken a call for six minutes. I then took another call.

11:05 - The wall boards, which are electronic signs on the wall displaying information on how many calls are waiting, flashed up with the slogan 'Don't get furious, get curious'. The phrase in itself made me furious.

11:58 - I have perfected the art of lying back in my chair and saying 'yes' every few seconds so the customer thinks I'm listening. When my latest call had ended, I did absolutely nothing for the customer and then pressed 'F8' to delete the customer's record from my screen. There are plenty of people in here with the same first name as me. They'll never know. I took another call.

12:14 - I answered a call by saying, "Can you get me a Twix", because John was going to the shop and a call came through unexpectedly. It's odds on that this will be the call they'll use in my appraisal to judge whether I get a promotion to Grade 2 pay scale (an extra 2p an hour).

12:30 - Lunch time. I went to the canteen which they have named 'the internet café', to make work seem less soul-destroying and ate my sandwich and then my Twix. Somebody was using the one computer they'd installed in the 'internet café' for the whole duration of my Lunch. They were on *www.jobs.co.uk*. I was still hungry so I looked in the overpriced vending machine they recently had installed in the canteen. I found it a bit strange that they had Braille on the buttons. Gary is registered blind and when he wants something from said vending machine, he has to ask what the code is for Beef crisps rendering the Braille redundant. Also, every time I go to the machine, the crisps are in a different place and that confuses *me* never mind Gary.

13:44 - No calls for ten minutes yet my team leader shouted at me for talking to John across the table. She said I should be reading my training manual. She might as well have hit me across the eyes with it she made me feel so disconsolate.

13:55 - Gordon tells me how he feigns interest in a customer's life by asking a question he knows will invoke a really long answer. He then presses the 'mute' button and looks at the BBC website until the customer says, "Hello?". He then presses mute once more and pretends he was listening all along before asking another intricate question.

14:23 - Gordon teaches me another skiving technique. When a call comes through, he presses mute. The customer is oblivious to the fact they are not in the queue any longer and so stay silent. Gordon said that if your call time reaches thirty seconds then it registers on the computer as a call taken and therefore on your statistics. He then hangs up on the customer. He takes 20 calls an hour and management think he's great. He's on a grade 2 pay scale.

14:44 - A customer called and said they wanted a new cupboard door. Before I could order a new one, I had to hold a yellow card in the air and get authorisation from a floorwalker who has worked here for three months. I've been here five years yet I'm not authorised to order a cupboard door. I've never felt so undervalued or unmotivated.

15:00 - My team leader printed off yesterday's statistics and told me that I needed to get my call time under three minutes. I tried to explain that when I get customers like I did this morning, a call takes as long as it takes to sort out – in that case thirty minutes. I asked if she wanted me to sort out the problem and give good customer service or cut the customer off when they've been on for three minutes. I'm now getting a disciplinary for non-compliance. It's my fault really, she did warn me.

15:06 - I pressed my 'not ready' button and waited for a minute, then turned it off and straight back on again so it only ever shows I've been 'not ready' for a minute. I'm doing it in protest at the appalling way I am being treated. Apparently someone using a computer somewhere else in the building can see that I've done this but there are hundreds of people who work here so I'll take my chances. There are two hundred calls in the queue now. I'm past caring and decide to stare out of the window at a man poking something on the ground with his walking stick.

15:23 - I logged out of my phone completely, I was so sick of my job. The reason being, I finally decided to take a call from a customer to alleviate the boredom but I couldn't find any notes on the customer's file. The only ones I could find said "Cus rang. Need inst for DB but see what has as diff was to build. Ring bk tues". I wondered why I'm here at all. I don't even think another Twix will help.

15:40 - My team leader asked why I was logged out. I didn't say anything and logged back in. I had to take calls as she was staring at me.

16:00 - I couldn't believe I'd still got another two hours of this to endure. I'm going to ask to move teams. They can talk between calls on Barry's team.

16:04 - I put my hand up to ask if I could go to the toilet but my team leader said no because John was on his break.

16:14 - I put my hand up to ask if I could go to the toilet because John was back from his break. My team leader said no because Colin was now on *his* break. Ironically I hadn't taken a call while I'd been waiting as there are none in the queue.

16:30 - It was finally my break. I think I've broken my kidneys.

17:00 - I'd been waiting for a call since I came back from my fifteen minute break. While I was updating my *Facebook* page (instead of reading a training file) my team leader poked me. I think she knew I was on *Facebook*. Hang on, that means she was too? I went on *Myspace* instead.

17:11 - My team leader asks if I have any WIPs; apparently this means 'work in progress'. She then tells me she wants them done by C.O.P.; this apparently means 'close of play'. Is her job so hectic that she has to shorten as many phrases as possible.

17:15 - I received a call about a sofa. I have a script to read from when I get a call about a sofa because I haven't been trained to take calls about sofas. I have told management this but they said, read this script to the customer. Surely it would be better for a customer to speak to someone who knew what they were talking about and could help them instead of someone reading off a bit of paper? I guess that's why I'll never be a manager in here. I deal in logic.

17:49 - Keith told me he thinks redundancies will be announced soon. He tells me about the last time they offered voluntary redundancies and got rid of twenty staff. Two weeks later they realised they had too much work and so offered those twenty staff their jobs back, explaining that they could keep their redundancy pay-offs. Keith would have got £20,000 but he thought it was too big a risk to take. Yet, he found himself sitting next to a guy who took his redundancy and then got his old job back with ten grand in the bank and a two week holiday for his troubles. As you can imagine, he hasn't had any enthusiasm for the job for a few months now.

18:00 - Finally the floor manager shouted "Lines are down" and everyone
logged out, except me as a call came through a second before he shouted.

18:24 - I was still on the same call and I'd missed *Can't cook, won't cook*. I don't get paid for this extra time – it's classed as 'needs of the business'. I won't even get the time back in breaks either. If I'm a minute late in the morning, they make me work back that minute in my lunch half-hour.

18:29 - I finally logged off and went home. My team leader threw me a disgusted look as she is not allowed to go home until I have logged off. Serves her right. I'm sure to be dragged in the office tomorrow for training as my last call of the day went over 3 minutes.

Customer Service Training

When you get a job in the service industry you receive what you'd expect to be specialist training; product, services, where the toilets are, that sort of thing. While this training is essential, a lot of call centres and smaller organisations send their staff on a course to improve what they call 'soft skills'. These skills include how to communicate effectively along with various team building exercises. The following is a list of the type of things that actually happen in these training sessions; bear these in mind when you're next writing a complaint letter or ringing a call centre.

1. Every trainee is given a sticker to put on their computer monitor which says, "Smile while you dial – don't moan when you phone". This makes none of them smile.

2. The trainer writes "What makes good customer service?" on an A1 flip chart pad in three different colours because the first two marker pens ran out. This instils the trainees' confidence in their trainer.

3. Twenty glazed pairs of eyes stare at the trainer blankly. Twenty pairs of ears hear nothing but white noise and twenty brains think about why they agreed to take the job in the first place.

4. The trainees get into pairs and sit back to back in an exercise which is supposed to prove that it's not what you say but the way you say it. However, they both find their minds wandering to what they're going to have for tea that night after doing the exercise twice and learning nothing.

5. Every trainee is placed into a team of 4-5 people and each group has to design a poster which demonstrates the importance of planning and organising in a customer service environment. No one wants the job of standing up and presenting their group's poster to the room. No one wants the job of writing on the A1 piece of paper with marker pens. No one wants the customer service job they accepted two weeks ago.

6. Six people fail to come back after the first break of the day.

7. The next exercise involves groups of 2-3 people doing a role play in front of the rest of the group which has no relevance to their jobs and is therefore limited in its value. The people doing the role play realise this and are even less enthusiastic than they were ten minutes ago when they nearly didn't come back after the first break of the day.

8. Those of the group who are still there, discuss what is meant by the word 'empathy', yet not shown how to put this word into action. The trainer deciding not to empathise with anyone in the room, deciding instead to continue talking about open and closed questions.

9. A brain-storming session is held, though the trainer calls it a *thought shower* and then calls it a *think tank* as she isn't sure what is politically correct and what isn't. After much deliberation she asks the group to '*blue sky*' some '*buzz-words*'. All but one of the words written on the A1 flip chart pad has come from the trainer's head. The one that didn't was 'burger' and really had no relevance to the prevailing topic of 'leadership skills'.

10. The smattering of agents left in the training session are inexplicably taught how to juggle. The trainer fails to mention why this is relevant.

11. The trainer thanks the trainee who stayed until the end for his time.

Write – don't phone

As outlined in 'a day in the life of a call centre agent', you're not always going to get the most favourable action to a complaint from telephoning the first line of customer service agents. It's possible that you will be passed to a manager, but this will be a manager who is responsible for customer service staff and not customer service *per se*. If you ring an organisation's head office, as opposed to the dedicated service centre, you may have more luck. Head office may well just direct your call back to the customer service centre, though it's likely your call will be taken by one of the dedicated 'head office' teams who deal with escalated complaints. However, it's much better to write than to phone and here's why.

1. In your incandescent state, you'll probably say something you regret.
2. A 'shouter' is more likely to find they've been cut off 'accidentally'.
3. Listening to a long list of dates, times and events is much like listening to the directions you get when you ask a passer-by where the train station is (you stop listening after the first two).
4. A telephone call isn't always recorded 'for training purposes' and service agents are often looking at E-bay rather than typing notes into your file such as when you rang and the reason for your call.
5. You can always go back and change what you've written in a letter before you send it (unless you've handwritten it and you've used permanent marker). You can't go back to a telephone conversation and change that four letter word you shouted so elegantly.
6. In a call that necessitates your talking for long periods, the person you're talking to will more than likely have the mute button pressed so they can talk to the person sitting next to them, only deactivating 'mute' to verbal nod you with a skilfully placed 'uh-hum'.
7. They will make you tell your protracted story only to advise you twenty five minutes later that you need to speak to a different department. Invariably, you will be patched through to the wrong department to whom you will relay your protracted story before being patched through twenty five

minutes later to a different department. Perpetually, you will be patched through to the wrong department.

In order to grab attention, we need to follow the advertisers' handbook. Give your letter some pizzazz. Clip art of a man with his hand stuck in a vacuum cleaner is good, as long as it is relevant to the letter. Photographs of what you're complaining about are good too – a picture of the slug you found in the bottom of your milk bottle or the hole in your garage roof left by the people who tried to deliver a skip to the flat upstairs for instance.

It is my view that the letter should be light-hearted and amusing. It engages the attention of the complaint handler and gives them a lift in their mundane day. From time to time however, customers unintentionally write things which are funny, but for the wrong reasons. These also give the complaint handler a lift and their power to help get the agent through the next hour at work must not be underestimated. The following phrases have been taken from genuine complaint letters I have personally dealt with in the past.

1. I came home to find the builder stripping the clematis from my back passage.

2. Ever since you fitted the central heating system I have had a leak in the bedroom, a leak in the living room and a leak in the bathroom.

3. I enquired last week about my missing mirror and you said you were looking into it.

4. Despite months of constant wear, my drawers are still stiff.

5. If you don't refund my Fridge Freezer in the next seven days I am calling the Police.

6. The boiler you fitted last month is very noisy. My wife and I are kept awake every night by the constant banging coming from our son's bedroom.

7. I think my cat might be under the floorboards.

8. I've had your engineer three times now and he hasn't satisfied me once.

9. The table was delivered to my mother with three legs.

10. As my boiler has broken down again, I am forced to use the kettle when I need a bath.

11. I can't tell you how frustrated I am. I want your inspector to come round immediately and sort me out or I will be forced to take legal proceedings.

12. After a few weeks, your assessor arrived, and in the presence of my sister-in-law, I was interrogated by his laptop for well over an hour.

13. I would say his grasp of English was to be not worthy of praise.

14. To add injury to insult, I burnt myself on the radiator.

15. The fitter said a six inch pipe was needed but my husband has assured me that four inches is quite adequate.

16. I am concerned about the integrity of my heating system as there seems to be an awful smell coming from the pump.

17. When my boiler fires up it sounds like "Ghosts".

18. I need the delivery charge refunded because my husband is due to have his feet pinned next week.

19. My suspicions were aroused when I witnessed the engineer putting his hand up my Mother's flue.

20. The cupboard has come away from the wall because my neighbour's twins insist on banging their balls against the side of my house.

When you send that letter of complaint, the company in question will hopefully write back. If you don't receive a reply within two weeks, then you should call them and ask to speak to the department that deals with correspondence. When you finally receive your response in writing, it will contain phrases which sound like they're taking your complaint seriously and you'll think you might actually gain the parity you so badly crave. Beware however, this letter is not what it seems. I have translated the most common phrases used by companies so you can see what they're *really* saying to you. Following that on page 70 is a template letter sent to most customers when they receive a complaint letter which has been annotated with translations.

Further to my previous letter dated 23rd January, I would like to apologise for the delay in responding but I am still waiting for the results of my investigation. (*I lost your letter, then found it two weeks ago, then forgot to reply and put it down the back of my computer and came across it when I was looking for that copy of Take a Break with the £1000 word search competition in it.*)

I apologise that our first response did not provide the information you required. (*I don't even know what was in the first letter you were sent. It was sent by the 'Temp' who's previous 'job' was 'community service'.*)

Should you have any further queries or concerns please do not hesitate to contact me. (*I never answer my telephone and I have told all the people who answer the phone in the call centre on my behalf to say that I am on leave at the moment.*)

Please accept my apologies for the inconvenience and any upset you have been caused. (*Hopefully you'll have absolutely no knowledge of the sale of goods and services act and you'll be sufficiently pacified by my hollow apology. Please don't take this to a solicitor.*)

I would like to thank you for bringing this to my attention, as we are always interested in feedback to enable us to make improvements in order to assist our customers. (*I hope you feel that even though you only got an empty apology, rather than the £3,000 compensation you asked for, your time hasn't been entirely wasted. Good job you don't know that once you stop ringing and writing in, your letter goes in the bin and not to some fictional department that takes customer's comments on board.*)

In order to demonstrate how sorry we are that you did not receive our normally very high standards of customer care, we would like to offer you an ex gratia payment of £300(*If I pay you £300 will you stop shouting at me and go away?*)

I trust that this is a satisfactory explanation. (*Don't bother writing again, that's all you're getting.*)

We may record or monitor calls for training purposes. (*We may record calls to find out which customer service agent is hanging up on customers when they've finally got through after negotiating six menus and a rendition of 'Land of hope and glory'.*)

With regards to the letter, which was sent to you by our offices, I would confirm that I was neither comfortable nor impressed with either the tone or the content of the same. I have dealt with this as a training issue and have taken the appropriate steps to ensure that there is no recurrence. (*We've sacked the 'Temp'.*)

I would also take this opportunity to assure you that as the Customer Response Manager, I will ensure that appropriate steps are, and will continue to be, taken to ensure that we strive for service excellence in all areas of our business.
(*We're now using a different 'Temp' recruitment agency.*)\

There is little comfort or resolution to be derived from apportioning blame for the delays incurred but I do believe it important to illustrate both that we believe both parties to be accountable, and that we have looked at identifying where the problems lay so we can prevent similar situations occurring in the future. (*We hope this sentence is sufficiently confusing that it sounds like we're actually doing something to help.*)

This remains an internal matter however and it will be dealt with accordingly. (*I'm not going to bother letting the department you've complained about know of your complaint. Even if I did, they wouldn't start washing their hands before they hand you your change from a £10 note.*)

We continually review all our customer's comments and, wherever possible, work to address these with our dealer network, in order that we may improve the services we both offer. (*I'm barely interested in writing this letter never mind looking up from my copy of Woman's Own long enough to 'review' your 'comments'.*)

Please be advised that your case has been investigated in detail, and the offer that has been made to you is purely a gesture of goodwill. (*It's compensation really but that word means admitting we're in the wrong and we don't want to do that now, do we? Please don't get a Solicitor involved.*)

Thank you again for taking the time to write to us and for allowing me the opportunity to clarify our stance in this matter. (*I hope you realise those ten minutes I spent writing this letter could have been spent watching people falling over on Youtube.*)

Please accept my apologies for this unusual and unfortunate situation. (*It is in no way unusual as I have used this line in every letter I have sent out so far today!*)

Your comments are noted and have been passed on to our Product and Marketing departments. There will always be areas of our marketing and production that are open to constructive comment and customer feedback such as yours. It is not only of paramount importance to us, but is also gratefully appreciated. (*I completely just made that department up – it doesn't exist. Now, four down, five letters, emotional state experienced during periods lacking in activity. 'B', something, 'R', something, 'D'.*)

The Template

This is an actual template used by the customer service department I worked in. The brief was to slightly change the wording in order to make it sound like a considered response when in fact, the same letter went out to every single complaint I dealt with. The references below explain exactly what the letter means.

Reference Number: 098/7653[1]

Mr Indiscernible
2 Any Street
Co. Mpensation
R3 4UND

23rd September 2008

Dear Sir/Madam[2]

Thank you for contacting us about your **broken spade**[3].

We are sorry that you feel unhappy with the service you have received[4] and can assure you that we take this matter very seriously[5].

Your complaint has been referred to our Customer Response Department[6] in accordance with the terms of the Company's Complaints procedure[7].
May we ask for your patience, as we will need to investigate the issues raised to answer your queries fully[8]. We will send you a response as soon as our investigations are complete[9].

In the meantime, please call us **on 0845000000**[10] if you have any other questions or concerns.

Yours sincerely,[11]

Nev R. Edit [12]
Client Relationship Manager

[1] To help us find you on our database of fifty thousand other customers who complained last week.

[2]This covers all possibilities (apart from that time a customer wrote in on behalf of her dog saying that the dog food wasn't in the slightest bit 'improved').

[3] This sentence makes the letter so personal doesn't it? The agent hasn't even realised he's typed the problem in the wrong font.

[4]Not really.

[5]Which is why we send the same letter to every customer who writes in, changing only a few words (see [3]).

[6]It's been passed from the person who opens the mail to the person sitting next to them who replies to the mail.

[7] Which we've had drawn up by a Sesquipedalian (person who uses big words) so that even when a customer requests a copy of it, they'll never find out how to successfully claim compensation.

[8]It's going on the bottom of a pile of five thousand other letters which are being dealt with slowly by the Managing Director's partially blind Aunty Maud. We ask for patience as it sometimes takes weeks for us to come up with an excuse for not giving you your money back.

[9] Which could be never, let's face it. We'll probably put it in the 'deal with if they ring in to chase' file.

[10] Spending 50p a minute being spoken to by a computer about how there's a sale on next Saturday.

[11] Not really.

[12] The person who earns the most money, does the least work and you can never speak to – even if you could, he'd transfer you back through to a new starter who doesn't even know who they work for.

ARE YOU CUT OUT TO WORK IN CUSTOMER SERVICES?

Looking for a new job? Think you see a future in the service industry? Then do this test to find out if you could work in customer services.

1. You're working in a call centre and your team leader shouts "Take a call". What do you do?

a) Flip your headset on enthusiastically and stare googly-eyed at the screen, ready to input a customer's details then go the extra mile to help.
b) Dial the *Odeon* film line and pretend you didn't hear.
c) Press a button on your phone which prevents a new call coming through and pretend you are typing some very complicated notes onto a customer's file.
d) Log out of your telephone and go on *e-bay* to buy a jigsaw.
e) Stand up, throw your headset at your team leader and storm out muttering to yourself about how you had more fun doing telesales.

2. You're working in a pet shop and you are approached by a customer who tells you the Rabbit they bought from you last week has a funny eye. What do you do?

a) Agree with the customer and talk about how terrible the situation is while trying to forge a path to mutual resolution.
b) Inspect the Rabbit and tell the customer to stop being so stupid – both its eyes are funny.
c) Shrug your shoulders, blow your cheeks out and say "These things happen".
d) Say nothing, walk away and get one of your more experienced colleagues to deal with the situation for you.
e) Say, "How is that *my* problem?", then go and have a cup of tea.

3. You are working in a Travel Agency and a customer asks if you have brochures on Skiing holidays. What do you do?

a) Sprint to the area of the shop where the brochures are, grab twenty of them and show the customer which pages in each brochure are relevant to their request.
b) Only show them the ones that make you the most commission.
c) Point out the brochures at the other side of the room and get back to filling in your Sudoku.
d) Say "I'm cruises" without making eye contact with the customer and continue to read the back of a bottle of correction fluid.
e) Say "We're a travel agency, what do *you* think?"

4. You work for a double glazing company. A client calls to say one of her units has condensation in it, two weeks after it was fitted. What do you do?

a) Empathise with the client and agree to send a fitter round immediately to fix the problem.
b) Explain that this problem will sort itself out and advise the client to call you back in six months if the problem persists.
c) Tell the client that you aren't the person responsible for this type of complaint and you'll get the manager to call back – then you don't.
d) Tell the client that the company who fitted the double glazing went bankrupt last week and changed its name so it's nothing to do with you.
e) Ignore the complaint and try and sell the client a conservatory with fifty per cent off (i.e. a conservatory that will always be half finished).

5. Where do you file your customers' confidential details for easy retrieval?

a) In a lockable filing cabinet, in alphabetical order with a chronological sub-filing system.
b) In a drawer by your desk in alphabetical order only.
c) On the floor.
d) They're confidential?
e) You'll file them when you've found a translator on the internet which can cope with the interesting website you've just found which is all in Chinese.

6. A customer calls and asks to speak to a manager. How do you handle it?

a) Explain that you are more than capable of resolving any issue the customer may have and then successfully resolve the complaint.
b) Pass the call to your manager.
c) Explain that your manager isn't available and ask the customer to ring back tomorrow.
d) Put the customer on hold until they hang up.
e) Ask the customer to hang on while you try and find your house on Google Earth.

7. One of the directors of the company is visiting your site today. What do you do when they make a joke?

a) Laugh sycophantically while clapping your hands and contorting your upper body at random angles.
b) Chuckle and wink provocatively.
c) Gaze around at the middle managers who are laughing sycophantically and vow you will never become one of them. Gaze back at your desk where you deal day in – day out with complaints then back at the director who made the joke and then laugh sycophantically along with everyone else.
d) Stand stony-faced and unmoved, possibly taking out one of the managers you don't like with a swivel chair.
e) Shout, "Can you stop being so unprofessional – I'm looking at pictures of people with Mullets on Google images and I can't concentrate!"

8. You are the manager of a customer service department in a large company. How do you run your team?

a) Providing sufficient training with structured working patterns and an attractive performance related pay structure to ensure each customer is handled professionally and efficiently.
b) Leave them to get on with it until their 'stats' start dropping then take them in an office and threaten them with the sack until they perform better or get another job.
c) Tell them all that it's how many calls they take an hour rather than the level of service they offer to each customer that is important.
d) Make your team deal with things they've never been trained to do and use it against them when it comes to a pay review.
e) Spend all your time in the canteen with other managers talking about who's got the worst staff, being particularly keen to name names and offer to swap one of yours for one of theirs. (You even use your most difficult member of staff as a make-weight in a game of Texas hold'em).

HOW DID YOU SCORE?

Mostly A's
You have an excellent attitude. Keep this up and management will pile so much work on you that the company will slowly consume your soul and you'll spend your latter years wondering where your dignity went.

Mostly B's
You're a good worker and you'll do as much as is asked of you. You are temperamental however and as soon as a job worth more money comes along, you'll be off.

Mostly C's
You really couldn't care less. You'll happily deal with customer queries but you will give the absolute minimum and wish you were somewhere else constantly.

Mostly D's
You really shouldn't be dealing with customers. Unfortunately, there are a lot of people like you working in the service industry.

Mostly E's
You have been sacked.

I want to complain!!

This section contains all the complaint letters I have written and their responses. There are complaint letters which I composed due to a failure of service by the company in question, in an attempt to gain parity or recompense. There are letters I wrote about things that annoyed me while fully aware that the letter may not change anything. There are also 'control' letters; they are frivolous but provide a vital balance when it comes to proving or disproving my assertion that light-hearted letters gain a more favourable response than angry ones.

1. Asda (1)
2. Asda (2)
3. Cadbury
4. Cineworld (1)
5. Cineworld (2)
6. Cineworld (3)
7. Golden Wonder
8. Kingsmill
9. Marks and Spencer
10. Nestle (1)
11. Nestle (2)
12. Newcastle City Council (1)
13. Newcastle City Council (2)
14. Old Orleans
15. Britvic
16. Pepscio (Walkers)
17. Sunderland City Council
18. Tesco (1)
19. Tesco (2)

ASDA 1

Paul Kelly
Director of Corporate Affairs
Asda House
Southbank
Great Wilson Street
Leeds
LS11 5AD

Dear Mr Kelly,

It is with a level of disbelief that I am writing to you regarding a
bizarre sequence of events which has reduced the likelihood of me
ever shopping in your Metro Centre store again to zero should this
situation not be resolved to my satisfaction.

As you will be aware, Sunday 19th December was a very busy day in
your store and I turned up there at 10:30am, attempting to avoid the
crowds and purchase all the food I'd need over the Christmas period.
However, half of the north-east of England also had this plan and I
found myself squashed up against the milk fridges for a good ten
minutes whilst I allowed a 'train' of trolleys to pass as I awaited my
opportunity to enter the aisle which contained condiments. Although
slightly irritated by this and many other similar episodes which
necessitated my standing pressed up against your fresh produce whilst
people struggled to negotiate the 'shelf stackers' with their 'dollies'
blocking 64.8% of the aisle allowing one shopping trolley at a time to
pass with 1mm clearance on each side, I remained calm. What I am
attempting to do here is set the scene of my frustration.

Upon reaching the check-out, I noticed two young lads dressed in the
colours of a local football team, Blaydon or someone, packing bags.
Now, I'm not against manipulating children for the benefit of the
greater good, but I don't want them to pack my bags. And so, after
placing all of the items in my trolley on the conveyor belt and reaching
the end of the check-out, I politely asked one of the boys to put down
the packet of frozen chips he was stuffing unceremoniously into a bag
and allow me to pack the bags myself. (Call me old fashioned but I
like to have the softer items at the top of the bags, rather than have two

2L bottles of fizzy pop placed on top of my hotdog buns, squashing them into what I can only describe as a 'collage').

Anyway, your less than cheerful check-out assistant managed to prise some ether from under her till, which turned out to be 'carrier bags'. These bags are thinner than my imagination can cope with. I'm sure it tells you somewhere on your enigma-coded receipt (enclosed) who the check-out assistant was, and if you ask her, she might remember me commenting to her that the bags were pointlessly thin and had to 'double up' on the larger items. The handles on three of the bags broke just as I put one item into them. I would love to exaggerate here but the truth goes way beyond any exaggeration I could come up with.

My events of my first complaint begin when I reached my car. Whilst lifting the bags into the boot of my car, the bottom of one of the bags split open sending several items onto the car park. These were

a) A bottle of Archers (£10) - smashed
b) Lamb curry (£3.46) – Split, most of the contents lying in the snow
c) Sweet and Sour Chicken (£3.24) – Split, all over the car park

There were no other items in this bag so don't tell me I 'over packed' it. Now, I understand we're in a very grey area here and I have lost almost £17 of shopping – what to do? Well, I thought, when I get home I'll write a very strongly worded letter to the manager to show my disgust at the state of the bags they provide (which I know has been subject to a feature on watchdog recently). It was when I got home and saw my receipt that blood really started to leak out of my eyes with anger. I have been charged for 2 bottles of Archers, when in fact I only purchased one. Not only was it smashed in the middle of your car park (which I had to clear up so I didn't burst my car tyres while reversing) but I had been charged £20 for the pleasure!!

You'll probably say 'you should check your receipt before you leave'. Yes, very easy to do when your shop is packed, kids from a local football team and sighing and staring at me thinking I am 'unreasonable' for not donating my money to their football club after spending nearly £100 on groceries (£10 of which on a ghost bottle of archers I will never taste) and being forced off the check-out as the assistant had already started bowling the next customer's items down the till before I'd even put my debit card away in my wallet.

How many people stand and look at their receipt, scrutinising it before they leave the till area? I wonder if this is your store policy and how many other people have been charged twice for items, because they've bought so much, they're not going to notice one more item on their receipt that shouldn't be there. How many other people have got home and noticed two of a high-priced item on their receipts and realised that they cannot now bring the matter up with the store? I cannot help but mention the irony of the store manager's name, 'Mr. Kitching!' The noise your tills are making if you are indeed instructing staff to put large items through twice to increase your profits?

At the very least I expect a refund of the £10 for the bottle of archers I didn't buy plus a further £17 for the items which were strewn on your car-park to be eaten by the seagulls which hang around, probably because they know that at any moment, someone else's bag is going to split and spread food all over the car park. I have copied this letter to Hugh Kitching (Store Manager) to see what he has to say.

One last thing, your website lists your address as 'Gibfide way' (it's actually 'Gibside way' – looks like your shop has moved? Or maybe you should change the shop's name to "AFDA"?

I'd like to wish you a merry Christmas but I'm going to wait and see what you do about this letter first.

Yours very unhappily,

Peter Nuttall

Mr. Peter Nuttall,

23rd December 2010.

Dear Mr. Nuttall,

ASDA STORES LTD
METRO RETAIL PARK
GIBSIDE WAY
METRO CENTRE
GATESHEAD
NE11 9YA
TEL: 0191 460 2981
FAX: 0191 461 9549

Thank you for your letter dated 20th December 2010. I was most concerned to learn of the problems you encountered on your recent visit to our store.

We aim to make our customers visits to our store as pleasant and trouble free as possible and I am sorry that on this occasion we let you down. One of the services we offer is assistance with bag packing. We also support our local charities and on the day of your visit a local football team was in to help with bag packing on this busy day. We instructed the footballers on the best way to pack bags and to always ask our customers if they wanted help with their packing. I am sorry that these instructions were not followed and that their bag packing frustrated and upset you. Our carrier bags have been designed to ensure they are strong enough to hold an amount equivalent to 15 tins of baked beans or 6 bottles of wine, however for heavier items we also offer stronger carrier bags which customers can buy should they wish. We were notified today that we had received a supply of faulty carrier bags in our store. It is impossible to identify the faulty bags purely by sight and we have briefed our checkout colleagues if they notice any issues with the bags to isolate the rest of the bags attached to that batch. The bags issued to you on your shopping trip failed to meet the required standard, please ask for myself or Janice Barron People Service Manager when you next visit the store and we will be only to happy to supply you with our bags for life free of charge.

I was sorry to learn that you were charged twice for your bottle of Archers at the checkout. It is important to us that our customers trust us and following your complaint I have taken this up with my checkout colleagues and everyone will take extra care when scanning items. I would like to assure you that this was a genuine error and it is never our intention to knowingly overcharge our customers. I would never instruct my colleagues to put large items through twice to increase our profits.

We recognise that providing legendary service is vital to our business and in retaining the custom and loyalty of our customers. I cannot apologise enough that this was clearly not your experience during your recent visit to the store. I am grateful to you for providing this valuable feedback.

Finally, thank you for informing me about the incorrect website address, I will make sure this is rectified as soon as possible.

I can appreciate how upsetting this shopping experience has been for you and I am very sorry for the concern and inconvenience caused. I have enclosed a £40 gift card by way of a further apology and I hope that we can look forward to serving you again soon.

Yours sincerely,

Hugh Kitching,
General Store Manager.
Asda Gateshead.

Registered Office: ASDA House, Southbank, Great Wilson Street, Leeds LS11 5AD
Registered in England No 464 777

ASDA 2

Sally Hopson
Retail Operations Director
ASDA Group Limited
Asda House Southbank
Great Wilson St.
Leeds
LS11 5AD

Dear Ms Hopson,

I am writing to complain in the strongest terms about the new manager of your store in Byker, Newcastle. I purchased a casual summer top on the 1st May 2008 for £8. After wearing it twice, I noticed the stitching coming away at the elastic at the back. One of the buttons had also fallen off the front, which I had to stitch back on myself. This again fell off; for £8 I suppose I shouldn't have expected any different. However, I would expect this garment to have lasted longer than 35 days so I spent a couple of pound in petrol driving to Byker to take this back for a refund (or at the very worst, a credit voucher). After speaking to the sales assistant, whose face did not change from a scowl throughout our conversation, she said that she would have to speak to the manager, a Mister Eugene Morgan, to see if they were allowed to refund the top as it was out of your statutory 28 day period. When she came back, she informed me that the manager did not see this top as faulty and refused a refund.

He refused to come out of his 'manager's den' to explain to me face to face why his eyes are blind to frayed stitching and missing buttons.

For a 'store manager' he has an appalling grasp of the Sale of Goods act – which clearly states that your 28 day policy does not constitute consumer law and therefore, I am entitled to my refund.

You may think £8 is a paltry sum to be quibbling over – tell that to the store manager who has now cost me not only the original £8 but also the petrol money and cost of a stamp to bring this frankly weird standard of customer service to your attention.

Having shopped at ASDA for 10 years, I have never had a problem (apart from that time a small child ran into me, knocking a frozen chicken out of my hand into the path of a large man with a beard who stood on it, slid into a larger man with a larger beard and knocked over the display of diet coke, which was on special, two bottles for two pound).

Your customer service staff are always helpful and project a very positive image for your organization. This incident however has tainted my view and has at the very least prevented me from stepping foot in your Byker store ever again. What happens the next time I buy something that doesn't meet legal standards?

I would like a positive response to this complaint in the form of a refund or at the very least, a credit note, to go some way towards restoring my faith in your service. I have enclosed the receipt as proof of my purchase. I do sincerely hope you will investigate this matter with the store in question as your manager is contravening consumer law by ignoring the sale of goods and services act. If I do not receive a sympathetic response, I will take this matter up with John Buxton, your General Manager, Simon Mitchell, your Brand Manager and Trading Standards among other consumer advice bodies.

Kind Regards,

Peter Nuttall

part of the **WAL★MART** family

Our Ref: 16302188

15 June 2007

Mr. Nuttall

ASDA Stores Ltd
ASDA House
Southbank
Great Wilson Street
Leeds LS11 5AD
Tel: +44(0)113 243 5435
Fax: +44(0)113 241 8980
Mincom: 0800 068 2003
www.asda.com

Dear Mr. Nuttall

Thanks for your recent letter about our Byker Living store.

I'm concerned to hear we didn't handle your complaint as well as we should have when you took your summer top back to the store. If any of our customers ever feel the need to complain we certainly want to put things right as soon as possible, and I'm very sorry this clearly didn't happen this time.

I'm surprised the top had become damaged so quickly. We pride ourselves on the quality and value of our George range. We'd expect them to last much longer and they usually do. I've passed on details of your experience to our George buyers so we can make sure our usual high standards are maintained.

I've also now spoken to Eugene Morgan, the general store manager. He was not aware of what happened to you and certainly didn't refuse a refund. As he said to me, our 28 days returns policy only applies when you change your mind and no longer want the garment. If it's faulty then you can return it with your receipt after that time.

He's told me he'll rebrief his team so mistakes like this don't happen again in the future. He'll also be writing to you with a refund for the top. In addition, I've enclosed a further gift card as an apology. Please don't leave us! I'm sure you'll have a much more positive experience if you visit the store again.

Thanks again for taking the time to let us know about this. I hope our response will go some way towards restoring your faith in us and we'll be able to welcome you back into one of our stores again soon. If there's anything else I can help you with in the meantime, please do let me know.

Yours sincerely

Sally Hopson
Central Operations Director

Enc. £10 gift card

Registered in England No. 464777
Registered Office,
ASDA House, Southbank,
Great Wilson Street, Leeds LS11 5AD

CADBURY 1

Consumer Relations Department,
Cadbury,
PO Box 12,
Bournville,
Birmingham,
B30 2LU

Dear Mr Cadbury,

Ever since I was a little boy I have been plied with alcohol without my knowledge. I would quite happily purchase tins of top deck (each containing 0.03% alcohol) and after downing 300 cans, find I was unfit to drive. The amount of wine gums I downed when I was young is untold, that's without the consumption of my sisters liqueurs at Christmas when she wasn't looking, vile though they were. Jelly pints of lager and champagne truffles didn't help either nor did Threshers having a copious selection of confectionary so elegantly placed near the £4 for 6 Kestrel! The daddy of all my (unwittingly) alcohol fuelled encounters with the social worker was your 'Old Jamaica' dark chocolate rum and raisin bar. Not four squares of chocolate had passed my lips before I was wrapping my arms around strangers and telling them they were my best mate. A chocolate bar so alcoholic, after just five squares I found I could set fire to my own tears. One time, I ate a whole bar and woke up tied to a lamp-post, naked save for a pair of underpants which were perched on my head. One plus point of this was the tolerance my liver and brain seemed to build up over time. With the introduction of Hootch (a tasty lemony alcoholic beverage designed to get kids to start getting legless), I found I could drink a full crate without losing my balance, WKD and Absinthe came and went. I even started snorting Jack Daniels to try and reach that euphoric state most people seem to reach after just one sip of Baileys. As *The Verve* once so rightly said 'The drugs don't work'. It is for this reason Mr. Cadbury, that I plead, nay urge you to reintroduce your chocolate with the Rum soaked raisins so I can once again get intoxicated without my knowledge.

I have made do with dipping my Wispa (which you so kindly reintroduced) in pure Ethanol to get by.

Yours disgruntledly,

PO Box 12 Bournville
Birmingham B30 2LU

Consumer Direct Line: 0800 818181
Switchboard: 0121 458 2000
Fax: 0121 451 4297

www.cadbury.co.uk

23 October 2008

Mr P Nuttall

Our Ref:- 1493211A

Dear Mr Nuttall,

Thank you for your recent letter.

Consumer preferences do change from time to time and as a major manufacturer it is important that Cadbury maintain a wide range of products that are in line with changing consumer demands. For this reason new products are regularly introduced and any line not matching up to expectation is withdrawn. Although this product has been discontinued, we do listen to consumers comments so there is a chance you may see it again in the future.

We have passed your comments onto our Marketing Department for their information.

Thank you for contacting us.

Yours sincerely

PM Lovell

PP Claire Prince
Consumer Relations Department

Registered Office: PO Box 12, Bournville, Birmingham B30 2LU. Company Number 155256

Peter Nuttall

CINEWORLD 1

Cineworld Customer Services,
Power Road Studios,
Power Road,
Chiswick,
W4 5PY

Dear Cineworld,

When I think of the word 'Cinema', it conjures memories of
yesteryear, a bloke at the front playing the piano while people fall over
in black and white and hang off clocks in an amusing way. The velour
curtains sliding, nay, *sweeping* majestically to the edges of the screen
as the lights fade. A time when the film would have an interval half
way through and a woman with a torch and a tray would mill randomly
around the cinema selling choc-ices for 5p (that's about 20p in today's
money), then when the film finished, you could just sit, wait for ten
minutes then watch the whole thing again for free.

Sadly, those heady halcyon days have faded into a murky yet somehow
golden past. These days, we are 'treated' to a 3D Dolby laser-disc
digital surround sound experience, a choice between arm-chair
Pullman seat luxury, spring loaded cushion pad technology or the wet
cardboard boxes down the front, little blue lights that line the aisles
guiding you to your seat in the dark and large burly security guards
making sure you don't take sweets into the cinema that were purchased
from someone other than yourself. It's comforting to know that these
'bouncers' are employed not to protect the public from nutters trying
to emulate their hero from the film 'Who got maimed this time III', but
to eject anyone who commits the heinous crime of secreting a packet
of *Polos* in their handbag, or a carton of *Ribena* about their person.

As I visited one of your capitalist Cineworld cinemas yesterday, being
charged the princely sum of £6.50 at peak times and £6.49 at off-peak
times (which is between the hours of 9am and 11am when the cinema
is shut), I entered the foyer and noticed the plethora of snacks and
beverages on offer. The first machine I encountered dispensed hot and
cold drinks. The first nozzle bestowed me with weak coffee, the
second with tea that tasted like coffee, the third was orange with bits of

coffee floating in it and the fourth was hot chocolate, which was actually coffee as you had run out of hot chocolate.

I then noticed a lady ordering a bucket of coke, a hot dog, 2 trays of nachos (one with salsa dip, one with garlic), a bucket of popcorn, a bar of chocolate, a tub of Hagen Dasz, a choc ice and a muffin. She promptly had a heart attack, not from the consumption of these high cholesterol foods, but from looking at the bill for her purchase. I prised the invoice from her still twitching fingers after administering the kiss-of-life, the six figure sum made even *me* a little faint, and I've got kids! My daughter has had to re-mortgage her hamster cage just to afford a tiny cup of your orange juice with an unnecessarily high proportion of ice.

I don't understand where this money is going? Your staff all look like they should really be at school studying 'the anatomy of arses and elbows', so they can't be getting paid much and the film industry hasn't come up with an interesting concept for a film since '*Pingu, the Movie*'. We inexplicably have to sit through the so called renaissance of the film industry which includes releases such as "*Miami Vice*" (a reworking of an old TV show) and "*Superman Returns*" (a reworking of an old film). Mystery and suspense is certainly alive with "*Poseidon*" (a reworking of an old film), "*King Kong*" (a reworking of an old film) and "Oh no, I think the world's gonna blow up, get Will Smith to help II" (The sequel to every film Will Smith has ever made). Do you wonder why DVD piracy is so prevalent? Movie producers have taken to making low-budget re-makes of recent releases such as 'Snakes on a plane', which they have renamed 'Snakes on a train'. I personally cannot wait for the sequels, '*Snakes on a mini-bus*', '*Snakes on a bike*' and '*Snapes on a plane*' in which Professor Snape from Harry Potter clones himself and charters a flight to Azkaban.

The fact you have a 150% mark-up on your food prices has left me with no option but to teach my children the dying art of Smuggling. It's only a short step from smuggling Truffles into a Cinema to wearing an eye-patch, cutting one of their legs off to replace it with a piece of discarded plinth from my recent kitchen refurbishment and saying 'ahaaar' before every sentence.

I ask you to please consider the fact that what used to be a relatively inexpensive way to entertain the kids on a Saturday afternoon has turned into something similar to being on the corkscrew at Alton towers – you are taking your customers for a ride! Let's hope you never employ ex-health care staff as the amount of people shuffling through your 'security' looking like they have abnormal 'growths' under their t-shirts will certainly set the alarm bells ringing. Why not go the whole hog and install airport x-ray machines to check the people coming through your doors and confiscate anything edible (which should include finger nails as these are eaten during moments of mild threat or horror)?

Yours thoroughly skint for the next 3 months,

Peter Nuttall

Outcome: I received no response to this letter and so wrote a second letter.

CINEWORLD 2

Cineworld Customer Services,
Power Road Studios,
Power Road,
Chiswick,
W4 5PY

Dear Mr Cineworld,

You have made me very sad. Not only have you, the second largest multiplex cinema chain in the UK, failed to respond to my complaint, you've also put your prices up. That's what is known in legal terms as a double whammy! As you might be aware, there is a credit crunch on and since my original complaint letter the value of my house has sunk lower than the cost of one of your buckets of popcorn. All I want to do is buy my Minstrels from the corner shop (89p) rather than your foyer (£2.80) and eat them while watching a film that cost me the business end of eight quid to see.

Please Mr Cineworld, reply to my original letter (enclosed) which I sent two months ago. I don't like feeling sad.

Yours sadly,

Peter Nuttall

Outcome: Still no response so I wrote a third letter

CINEWORLD 3

Cineworld Cinemas Head Office
Power Road Studios
Power Road
Chiswick
London W4 5PY

Dear Mr Cineworld,

We meet again – well, not actually meet, but I've written to you twice before and you ignored me. I'm hoping that my third letter might get at least a 'sorry for the inconvenience' or a 'stop writing to us you annoying twit'.

My tale takes us to your wonderfully expensive Cinema in Boldon, Tyne and Wear. As you know, I regularly smuggle food in as yours is very pricey. I have to sellotape packets of M+M's to my kids ankles and make them wear thick socks for fear that I will be refused entry for not paying £2.99 for a packet from you when the shop near my house sells the same ones for 60p. Anyhoo, my children were very excited about seeing the latest offering from *Pixar*, entitled "Up". I was less excited than them as it took me back to a moment in my childhood when a balloon seller asked me to hold his stock while he tied his shoelace. It took firemen 3 hours to get me down from the church roof.

I approached the sales desk and was greeted with a grimace from a young lad who regretted putting 'cinema ticket seller' on his work experience form the week earlier. "Two adults and two children for 'up' please", I said. Your sales clerk asked whether I would like to see this film in 3D. I considered this for a while; most things in my life are 3D you see, except things that are written down, and that was solved by the invention of the 'pop-up book' which didn't really enhance my life. My kids really wanted to see it in 3D however so I paid my money – over £20 – and was then mugged for an extra £2.50 per pair of 3D glasses! Were it not for the looks on my cherub faced kids, then I would have said a naughty word. Instead, I handed over another tenner in return for the least fashionable pair of glasses I've ever seen! I should have gone to Specsavers!

Maybe I'm being a little harsh – I enjoy the whole cinematic experience, which is why I keep paying over the odds to go to your cinema, and it can only be enhanced by things protruding from the screen and nearly poking me in the eye, can't it? Wrong! The film started and looked exactly like a 2D film. Instead of the screen being 50 meters away, it looked like it was only 45 meters away. "This is worth £2.50", I thought to myself sarcastically. Nothing protruded from the screen, nothing felt like it was whizzing past my nose, except for the boring bit in the middle when my kids decided to have a popcorn fight. In the end, I enhanced my enjoyment by taking off the glasses and watching a fuzzy screen as it was more fun trying to guess what was going on.

This all sounds very negative I know, but I haven't got to the good part yet! The film finished. Nope, that's still not the good part. We left the cinema to be faced with a woman holding a box, attached to which was a sign saying 'recycle your 3D glasses here'. Not only have you charged me £2.50 for them already, you want to pretend that when I give you them back, you're going to put them into some big 'glasses mashing' machine and turn them into paper for the homeless and save the planet? No, your version of recycling is to put them back in their packet and sell them to the next audience for £2.50 a pair making yourself a profit of - £2.50 per pair per film! Just how many other people had worn the glasses before me? If I get Swine Flu, I'm knocking on *your* door Mr. Cineworld!!

Speaking to a likeminded individual outside your cinema, I learned that even if I take my glasses home and then bring them along to another 3D showing, I am not allowed to use the glasses again, I must pay you ANOTHER £2.50, even though I already have!!!! Explain yourself in language the general public and trading standards can understand.

Thank God the car park is free.

Yours disgruntled,

Peter Nuttall

C I N E M A S

Unfortunately we will be unable to reimburse you on the surcharge you have previously paid; I have enclosed 4 pairs of 3D glasses for your family to use on your next visit.

Yours sincerely

Samantha Clarke
Cineworld Customer Services

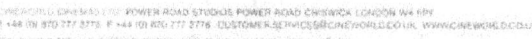
CINEWORLD CINEMAS LTD, POWER ROAD STUDIOS, POWER ROAD, CHISWICK, LONDON W4 5PY
T +44 (0) 870 777 2773 F +44 (0) 870 777 2776 CUSTOMER.SERVICES@CINEWORLD.CO.UK WWW.CINEWORLD.CO.UK
REGISTERED IN ENGLAND NO 5172376 REGISTERED OFFICE: 90 HIGH HOLBORN LONDON WC1V 6XX

REGISTERED IN ENGLAND NO 5172376 REGISTERED OFFICE: 90 HIGH HOLBORN LONDON WC1V 6XX

GOLDEN WONDER

GW Trading Ltd,
Customer Service Department,
Colin Road,
Scunthorpe,
South Humberside,
DN16 1TT

To Golden Wonder,

Your crisps have always had a place in my heart. Not literally you understand, as this would probably cause a myocardial infarction and let's face it, none of us want that! No, I am talking of the happy memories that dance playfully around my head whenever I hear the words 'Golden Wonder'. Your overcooked potato snacks are second only to 'Tudor' in my 'Crisp-Nostalgia' chart.

I had my first run-in with a crisp manufacturer when Walkers decided to change the colour of the bags of different flavours. Traditionally, Salt and Vinegar has always been sold in blue bags, cheese and onion in green and ready salted in white. They, in their wisdom, started putting Salt and vinegar in green bags and Cheese and onion in blue. It caused so much confusion, I found myself buying Panda pop and swizzle sticks too. This prompted me to go on a crusade to end this debacle but it ended in tears, mainly because I opened a bag of Pickled Onion Discos too close to my eyes, but I also failed to make any impression on the corporation that likes Gary Lineker so much.

This time, it's personal!!

You have recently re-introduced XL Cheese. I can only imagine it was the power of an e-mail such as this that made the boys in your marketing department decide on such a coup d'état. What they failed to notice, even through your extensive market research, is that no one likes cheese! Not even mice. You put a bit on a mouse trap – they just walk on past, grab a piece of lightly grilled smoked gammon, a glass of fruity white wine and a tray of Profiteroles – they ignore the cheese. Cheese smells like – well, cheese!

I was relaxing at work the other day in what they have aptly named 'The Internet Café', even though you're not allowed to eat anything in there but the confectionary vended from the machines therein. All of a sudden, the door burst open and a stampede of new starters piled in, clambering over those who'd fallen in their endeavours, those who will never again seek the crisps with the XL symbol. This commotion was followed by an even greater wind of gasps of disappointment which gusted through the air like a small tornado – Possibly an F2 (If you are familiar with the Fajita scale against which tornados are measured). The XL symbol was accompanied by the word 'Cheese'. Watching the ravenous rabble slink out of the door empty mouthed reminded me of my hungry childhood, where between meals, I had to gain nourishment from eating chewing gum off the road (only eating pink as this generally still had flavour).

This all brings me to ask, why have you not brought back XL Barbeque Beef?? Is it to tease me into sending this letter? Is it because there is a national cow shortage? A shortage of the letter 'B' perhaps or is it because a little bird told you that cheese is nicer than beef (not that birds eat cheese or Beef – except Vultures and they're not little)? Would you have a Cheese joint for your Sunday lunch? Would you have gravy on your feet-smelling cheese sandwich?

How could you do this to me? I like to fall asleep on my desk at work but this whole situation is keeping me up at day. It's now the major topic of conversation in the pub on a Wednesday, Friday, Saturday and Sunday night (and Saturday afternoon), from 'should we have tequila followed by lager or a Guinness followed by a Jack Daniels' to 'what extremes would you go to for a bag of XL Beef Barbeque crisps'. I have taken the liberty of listing some of the lengths my friends would go to, to get a bag :

1. Crawl over hot cigarette ash to the jukebox
2. Sit on one of the toilet seats in the Pig and Whistle
3. Listen to a whole song by Celine Dion
4. Snog Davy Henderson (and he's got scabs on his lips)
5. Go without tequila for a whole hour

After years of bombarding Nestle to re-introduce the cumbly-chocolated chewy-heaven that is the Texan bar, I feel it is your duty to bring back the national treasure that is XL Beef Barbeque crisps. As the crisps are so gorgeous, my colleagues and I have all agreed that you have to eat them in quantities of 3 packets at a time – therefore you would sell more, which in turn would boost your profits, thus securing your monthly bonus and a superb Christmas party – with a buffet consisting of XL Beef Barbeque Crisps, fine smoked Gammon lightly drizzled with fruity white wine, pan fried mouse, followed by profiteroles.

Oh and while I'm on, can you tell me what a crisp burns to?

Yours truly,

Peter Nuttall

GW Trading Limited

Cottage Beck Road
Scunthorpe
North Lincolnshire
DN16 1TT

Telephone: 01724 281222
Facsimile: 01724 292704

Mr P Nuttall

Date: 22/10/2008

Dear Mr Nuttall,

Thank you for your letter enquiring whether XL Beef Barbeque will be back in production.

We stopped producing XL Beef Barbecue due to lack of sales. However if we received enough demand for a certain product we will produce it. We re-introduced Ringo's due to an online petition been started.

Hope this information helps, and thank you for supporting our products.

Yours Sincerely

Bradley Hicks
Consumer Services Department

KINGSMILL

Kingsmill Careline,
Vanwall Road,
Maidenhead,
SL6 4UF

Dear Kingsmill,

Since the birth of bread around 8000 BC when the Egyptians crushed their grain by hand and baked their equivalents of today's chapattis, to the birth of agriculture in Britain around 1050 BC where barley and oats were grown freely, the first mechanical dough-mixer invented by the Romans in 150 BC, the windmill being invented by the Persians in 600 AD, King John introducing the first laws governing the price of bread in 1202, Chaucer's 'The miller's tale' which charted the greedy nature of Bakers (his opinion not mine), the great fire of London being started by a Baker (do you sense a theme here?), the best thing ever apparently being sliced bread after Otto Rohwedder invented the bread slicing machine, the abolishment of the 'National Loaf' in 1956, to the introduction of the 7p loaf in 1999 – no one has used as much flour on their baps as you!

Not only does it bring back horrific childhood memories of being forced to eat chalk when I pushed Tom 'Slap-bag' Higgins in the Nature pond at school, and the memory of sitting next to Darren Sanderson (who had a severe case of dandruff) in Physics, it's just not right! If I enjoyed eating dust, I wouldn't have bothered buying a vacuum cleaner. It may give your buns the appearance of the snow-capped mountains of Tibet, or all the grandeur of a bald head that a seagull has recently jettisoned its fully digested lunch over but is it at all necessary? There must be some kind of baking legislation governing the bread to flour ratio? I have had to stop wearing lipstick, for the sake of looking like a less feminine Marilyn Manson when taking a bite of my Kingsmill BLT.

I recently ate one of your buns in my car with the air conditioning on, the scene was akin to a snow globe from which there seemed no escape as the location of the door handle, air conditioning button and my own face remained a mystery for a good ten seconds. I was rescued by a passing tourist who mistook the inside of my car for a local monument (as is the norm inside snow globes). Me and my partner have started having competitions to see who can eat the most Kingsmill baps without choking to death owing to the moisture removing effect your flour has on our mouths.

I do sincerely hope you consider my complaint earnestly and perhaps you could give some of your excess flour to the Metro-Centre (my local shopping complex) to use as snow for this years Christmas decorations, and come to think of it, the next 28 years decorations.

Yours Faithfully,

Peter Nuttall

Ref: 4166636

17/10/2008

Mr Peter Nuttall
████████
████████
████████

CONSUMER SERVICES
Kingsmill Place, Vanwall Road
Maidenhead, Berkshire SL6 4UF

Dear Mr Nuttall,

Thank you for taking the time to contact us regarding your purchase of Great Everyday Soft White Rolls that we bake.

We understand you found the product to contain too much of the flour dusting, for which we would like to apologise.

We have reported this to the bakery concerned and they are carrying out an investigation into the matter. All necessary action will be taken to prevent a recurrence. Allied Bakeries are constantly striving to maintain the quality our customers both deserve and expect and we are sorry to have disappointed you on this occasion.

Please find enclosed vouchers to the value of £3.00, which we would like you to accept as reimbursement for the product and any costs that you may have incurred.

Again our thanks for your courtesy in drawing this matter to our attention.

Yours sincerely,

Jodie Miller
Senior Consumer Service Advisor

here to help

MARKS AND SPENCERS

Customer Service Department
Marks & Spencer
Chester Business Park
Wrexham Road
Chester
CH4 9GA

Dear Sir/Madam,

I have been buying your Sultana granola yoghurts for ages now and enjoyed every single one (because they all tasted the same) of them until last week, when I purchased two (one for now, one for later) from your store in the Metro Centre, Gateshead. Unless you have introduced a new secret ingredient (sand) into your yoghurt to enhance the texture, I think I've had two from a bad batch. The yoghurt was 'grainy' and a bit 'dusty' and tasted weird. Perhaps the cow from whence the yoghurt came had been eating the soil as well as the grass? I threw this out thinking it was just a bad one – then opened the other one and it tasted exactly the same.

I have enclosed the writing from the packaging so you can identify the batch or whatever you do on these occasions. Needless to say, I enjoy your yoghurts so much that I will probably buy another soon, hoping for it to be grit-free, so I'm not looking for the 'valued customer' stuff that you put in your letters of apology to consumers – your food section is far too perfect for that – but I *am* around £2.50 out of pocket.

I will leave the rest up to your imagination.

Yours faithfully,

Peter Nuttall

MARKS &
SPENCER

Retail Customer Services
Chester Business Park
Wrexham Road
Chester
CH4 9GA

Tel: 0845 302 1234
Fax: 0845 302 0116
marks-and-spencer.com/help

Mr Peter Nuttall

Our Ref: 1-232865159
30 July 2009

Dear Mr Nuttall

I am sorry to hear that you were disappointed with the quality of the yoghurt you bought from us recently.

We always appreciate any customer feedback which will help us to identify where we can still improve a product, so thank you for bringing this to our attention. It seems that despite our rigorous quality controls with our supplier we have not met expectations on this occasion. I will ensure that the Food Department is informed. I know they will investigate and take steps to make sure the highest standards are being met.

I would like you to have the enclosed gift card to the value of £3.00 as a refund, which comes with my best wishes.

I hope that future purchases of your favourite yoghurts do not disappoint!

Thanks for getting in touch.

Yours sincerely

Stephen Duxbury
Customer Adviser
Retail Customer Services

Marks and Spencer plc
Registered Office:
Waterside House
35 North Wharf Road
London W2 1NW
Registered No. 214436
England and Wales

NESTLE 1

Customer Services Manager
Nestle UK Ltd,
(Registered Office),
St. George's House,
Croydon,
Surrey,
CR9 1NR

Dear Nestlé,

I am sure you have had many e-mails, letters, phone calls and people standing outside your factory with little placards chanting 'Bring back the old smarties tube'. I understand that when something you've grown up with, something that has formed the cornerstone of society for over 50 years, changes – well, as you can imagine, society itself can crumble. Now, I am not a traditionalist, I don't hanker for those heady days when you'd forget what the letter 'a' looked like so you went out and bought 50 tubes of smarties in the hope there'd be one on the lid (even though there was one in the title printed on the side). Nor do I pine for that halcyon past when life was easy; those coloured sweets reminding me of a better time when people could just leave their front doors open and we'd all huddle round the coal fire – something we wouldn't have had to do if we'd just shut the front door! I don't even sit in the corner, rocking and staring at the wall, wishing things didn't have to change, wishing I could go into shops again and ask for a Marathon and not get funny looks, any more. But I suppose that change is inevitable, except from car park ticket machines.

No, I am not one of those people. Yes, the packaging has changed, no doubt cheaper to make, no doubt holding less smarties and no doubt creating a furore so large that it markets your product for you! I understand the health and safety angle; many's the time my class mates at school started clawing at their throats because they swallowed the lid, mistaking it for chocolate. Also, using the lid as a missile and flicking it off the top of the tube almost always ended up with a classmate ending up in the eye hospital. I am not stupid Mr Nestle, I understand that because you can't re-seal the new tube like you could with the old one, it means you have to eat all the smarties in one go, increasing the frequency of buying replacements and increasing sales. I can also assure you that the presenters of Blue Peter are not happy with you either. They are now on the lookout for something else they can make into a telescope. Also, my son has Aspergers Syndrome and Smarties are his favourite sweet, but he said he will never buy another tube unless the shape of the tube is changed back; he used to use the tube as an escape tunnel for his micro machines.

While I was at school I used to pretend I had a sprained ankle to get out of Physical Education. Our PE teachers, would double up as English teachers and the like, so in order for me to remember to limp, I put a Smartie lid under my foot, in my shoe. It worked a treat, and limp I did. I got out of PE alright - in fact it worked so well, I was off school for the following two weeks as I had an enormous blister on the bottom of my foot, with the letter d on it. It could have been a p or even a q, it depended on what angle you looked at it from. Children everywhere are now going to be subjected to monkey bars and Rounders against their will.

None of these things concern me however but what does boil my boots is that I have nowhere to put my 20p's!! With the old tubes, I could tell straight away when I had saved up £15. Now I have to *count* my money! DO YOU THINK THIS IS ACCEPTABLE??? This is where you have failed me Mr Nestle, my finances are now in chaos thanks to you. I have a mind to copy this e-mail to the government – if you won't bring back the circular tube, maybe they will make 20p's hexagonal?

MY LIFE IS IN RUINS! My wife is now having an affair with the next door neighbour, my cat has got flu, the kids in the back street have hidden my wheelie-bin and I have nowhere to put this weeks rubbish, I'm having a bad hair day and on top of all this, I HAVE 20p's STREWN WILLY-NILLY ACROSS MY DRESSING TABLE!! I hope you're happy with yourself Mr Nestle, when I'm gone, I'm going to haunt you! I WANT COMPENSATION!

If I am not properly compensated, I'm going to tell your boss you hit me.

Kind Regards,

Peter Nuttall

Nestlé UK Ltd

YORK YO91 1XY

Telephone 01904 604604
Facsimile 01904 804534

Register with Nestlé for the latest
product news & special offers
www.nestle.co.uk

Mr Peter Nuttall

DIRECT LINE 0800 000000

DATE

DIRECT FAX 01904 600000

002240481A   22 October 2008

Dear Mr Nuttall

Thank you for getting in touch about Smarties we really enjoyed reading your very amusing letter.

With any change to a long established and much loved product there are bound to be loyal users who feel upset.

Smarties have been available in markets throughout Europe for many years now, starting in the UK in 1937. We are, however, always looking at ways to improve our products to give more to the consumer in terms of both taste and value for money and we are obviously concerned to maintain the highest possible standards for our products. This was the first ever change to the traditional Smartie tube.

We are aware that people had lots of fun with the tube and the plastic lids however, the new hexatube is a great development for Smarties, the flip-top lid is resealable and we will be placing quirky messages, stickers or images on the flip-top lid.

I hope this explains some of the reasons for the change. I am enclosing 4 empty old style tubes for you and also the new Smarties Hexatube which I hope you will enjoy with our compliments.

Thank you again for taking the trouble to contact us. We are grateful for the interest you have shown in our Company.

Yours sincerely

Joan Emmerson
Consumer Relations Executive
Consumer Services

NESTLE 2

Customer Services Manager
Nestle UK Ltd,
(Registered Office),
St. George's House,
Croydon,
Surrey,
CR9 1NR

Dear Mr Nestle,

You may or may not remember that you ruined my life not so long ago by changing the tubes on your Smarties but more than made up for it by sending me 4 old style tubes to keep my 20p collection in order. You know what they say, if there's order in your change, there's change in the order. I don't know who 'they' are, but I believe them. Once my 20p's were neatly stacked inside the cardboard cylinders you sent me I thought that would be an end to my troubles. How wrong I was Mr Nestle, how wrong I was.

This morning, as I am on a strict diet (which I got from someone who wrote a book that I've never met or heard of), I only bought two packets of Discos and a Kit-kat. I like Kit-kats so much, I started supporting York City football club. I had a suggestion that you start manufacturing crescent shaped Kit-kats and sell them on Kit-kat crescent but as your sponsorship deal expired in 2010 this is not only a terrible idea, it has also made me wonder why I'm standing watching non-league football. However, I digress – like many people who purchase your four-fingered version of the chocolaty wafer based confectionary, I slid the bar (covered in the thinnest foil science is able to manage) from the red and white paper wrapping, coursed my fingernail down the groove between the first and second finger and then lightly snapped the finger from its nearby cousins. I then removed the foil (please stay with me, this is all relevant) from the finger and bit into the first 3mm at the end. I have four ways of eating the fingers, one for each finger – I will list them below :

1. Nibble the 1mm of chocolate from the edges leaving just the wafer with chocolate on the top and bottom, then scoff it down.
2. Take 3mm bites all the way down the shaft until the finger has gone.

3. Snap the finger in half and eat each half whole (if that makes sense).
4. Put the entire finger in my mouth so it pokes into both my cheeks and then use my tongue to snap the finger and scoff it all down.

Now, I'm sure I'm not the only customer of yours who has this common habit (I have tried all 4 methods with your Kit-kat chunky, ending up in the dental hospital with three of the methods and the eye hospital on the fourth) but when it came to eating the first finger of Kit-kat this morning I nibbled at the end and removed the chocolate but I did not reveal the edge of a wafer. I nibbled again – again no wafer's edge. I nibbled and nibbled and nibbled – no wafer. What exactly do you think you're playing at? A Kit-kat with no wafer is like a T4 presenter who isn't annoying. It's like someone who organised a jumble sale who doesn't need life coaching. It's like pulling a cracker that didn't go bang, the hat was ripped, the toy was broken and the joke wasn't funny. It's like square Beef Hula-hoops made out of fists that punch you in the temples when you open the packet.

It seems your staff is removing the wafers for their own personal use. Perhaps they are selling them on e-bay as 'naked Kit-kats'? This is an OUTRAGE.

Or is it?

Strange as it may seem – I rather enjoyed it without the wafer. I am now conflicted as to whether to complain about the fact there was no wafer in my Kit-kat or complain that you don't make a product which is purely 4 chocolate fingers.

If you have a heart, you'll help me here. I'm scared.

Yours incandescent/confused,

Peter Nuttall

Nestlé UK Ltd
YORK YO91 1XY

Register with Nestlé for the latest
product news & special offers
www.nestle.co.uk

Mr Peter Nutall

DIRECT LINE/ 0800 000030

DATE

DIRECT FAX 01904 603401

002874746A   7 April 2011

Dear Mr Nutall

Thank you for getting in touch about Kit Kat.

We are sorry your bar had no wafer and hope you may be interested to know how these bars are made. The wafer is placed into a liquid chocolate mould. The machine sometimes jams and we miss a centre so the whole mould fills up with chocolate. If this happens, we try to reject all the solid bars but, very occasionally, one will slip through. However, I am fairly certain that there is no 'nude' Kit Kat Ebay racket taking place and our team in the factory would not dream of such a thing.

We take great pride in producing really good products and can assure you our quality standards have not changed. We work hard to prevent problems like this happening so that your Kit Kat break can be as enjoyable as possible. I might add that although your technique of eating Kit Kats using the 'tongue snap' method is unusual, it is also potentially high risk and I would seriously consider the safety issues before eating any more.

Thank you once again for taking the trouble to contact us. We have enclosed a contribution towards your next purchase and hope you enjoy our products for many years to come.

Yours sincerely

Stuart Jones

Nestlé Consumer Services

NEWCASTLE CITY COUNCIL 1

Complaints Officer,
Democratic Services,
Civic Centre,
Barras Bridge,
Newcastle upon Tyne,
NE99 2BN

Dear Newcastle Council,

The holiday season is upon us and filling in the summer holidays can be challenging! You can imagine my excitement as I strapped myself in and held on as I was taken on a white knuckle, brown-underpant ride - my stomach performing somersaults and my eyes literally being forced from their sockets with the g-force. No, I didn't go to Alton Towers, I took a five minute ride in one of your hackney cabs! Being his livelihood, you'd expect the taxi driver in question (Registration *** *** - driving the ******** *******) would do everything in his power to keep his driving licence, however, this driver seemed to want to do anything he could to lose it. On entering the vehicle outside central station, I was met with loud R+B music which not only contained extremely offensive profanities but also drowned out where I'd like to be taken (the driver deciding to ask me three times where I wanted to go rather than turn the music down). So we set off - my life flashing before my eyes as we topped 40 miles per hour before we'd even left the car park. On the main road, a driver in the right hand lane indicated in ahead of our car - my driver took unexplainable umbrage to this action and sped up. Maybe his masculinity was being thrown into question by someone wishing to join his lane? He then gave a three second continual honk on the car horn and described the driver in front rather fruitily using words he'd learned from his CD player.
We then proceeded along the road no more than the width of an ant's leg away from the driver who had legally pulled in front of us. I'm not entirely sure what our driver was trying to achieve as the technology has not yet been developed to emulate wacky races where the car lifts up, leaving the wheels on the road so you can drive over the car in front. The car in front decided not to move out of the way so our driver moved into the left lane and undertook the car in front (in a 50 miles per hour limit) at 80 miles per hour. Every other speed limit was

ignored (all to a soundtrack of swearing rappers) even as we waited at traffic lights, I felt like we were doing at least 40. I asked the driver to stop well short of where I live so I could take the number plate (should he see me doing this, he may know who it was who complained about him). I have had to leave this letter anonymous as the character of the driver suggested to me that he would seek some reproach should this letter have any effect on his employment (not that it would because I have no evidence that any of these events occurred). Maybe you are that driver? In which case, I have also copied this letter to the Police - unless you are the police? In which case I should just be thankful that I am still alive.

Yours Nervously,

Peter Nuttall

Newcastle
City Council

S.P. Savage
Director of Regulatory Services and Public Protection
Environment and Regeneration Directorate
Civic Centre, Newcastle upon Tyne, NE1 8PB
Tel: (0191) 232 8520, ext. 23853   Fax: (0191) 278 3851
E-Mail: rspp@newcastle.gov.uk   www.newcastle.gov.uk

Our Reference: RSPP/LIC/GJHS/

Your Reference

Please address any correspondence regarding this matter to:
Licensing Office,
Regulatory Services and Public Protection,
Newington Road East,
Newcastle upon Tyne   NE6 5BD

This matter is being dealt with by Mr. G.J.H. Smith, extension 23853

29 October 2008

Peter Nuttall

███████
███████
███████

Dear Sir,

Hackney Carriage Registration Number : ███████████

I write in response to your letter explaining the circumstances of a journey you have undertaken in a vehicle bearing the registration number ███████████

I have checked our records and can find no vehicle with this registration number which is licensed as a hackney carriage with this Authority. This sort of behaviour of a driver falls way below the standard expected as a fit and proper hackney carriage driver and I would have been willing to take the appropriate action against the driver if licensed to drive by Newcastle City. Unfortunately I can take no action on this occasion. I will however instruct the enforcement team to try and locate this vehicle and take any action appropriate if operating illegally.

I thank you for bringing this matter to my attention.

Yours faithfully

Senior Licensing Officer

Services Provided:
Taxis and Street Trading
Contaminated Land
Dog Warden
Resilience Planning
Food Safety

Health and Safety
Building Control
Animal Health
Liquor Licensing
Parking Control

Pollution Control
Private Sector Housing
Gambling Licensing
Street Scene Enforcement
Trading Standards

NEWCASTLE CITY COUNCIL 2

Complaints Officer,
Democratic Services,
Civic Centre,
Barras Bridge,
Newcastle upon Tyne,
NE99 2BN

Dear Sir,

I am writing for a number of reasons, which will become clear as this letter progresses. The first of said reasons is to tell you what happened to me and my fiancé on Saturday evening, **[th] September 2007. We arrived in Newcastle city centre by car and wondered where to park, as Newcastle has a plethora of parking options. We decided to park as we most often do, in the multi-storey car park on Dean Street. We chose a bay near the entrance, (which for the benefit of the latter part of this letter, was one parking space away from the parking attendants office) and I got out to purchase a ticket to enable us to park legally in your conveniently located car park. I placed a pound coin in the slot at 17:22 (which is 5:22 pm in the evening on the 24 hour clock). This payment of one English pound enabled us to cheerfully wander the streets, as long as we returned to our vehicle by 19:28 (that's 7:28pm) without incurring a penalty. As the bay we chose was one away from the office of the man who ambles around checking the cars, it had not crossed my mind that I should be concerned about the fee asked of me. Though I have recently secured a pay rise at work which certainly helped to cover that 'one pound' parking fee, having just paid £30 for petrol (which got me around 1 litre), I thought risking a parking fine of £30 (or £60) was perhaps on this occasion a little foolhardy, given that the man who had the power to invoke this fine was but 3 steps away from the car, reading the paper and listening to Radio 4 in his warm office, which I notice also had a kettle – no doubt to provide him with an interminable supply of Cadbury's Options and Horlicks. I decided not to take the risk of hoping the Horlicks would take it's effects and send the attendant into a slumber long enough to keep that precious pound coin in my pocket and not in your machine.

Anyway, I placed my coin in the machine; the ticket I received told me that we didn't have to return to the car for around two hours and so off we went. After a thoroughly nice evening, we returned to find a parking ticket on the windscreen of the car. Confused, I took the plastic wallet from the glass, via the least sticky piece of red sellotape in existence (I suggest you review this and up the parking control department's budget on sticky-backed plastic) and investigated. Just as an aside, I also notice that you haven't yet discovered the technology that other car parks now use as standard which have a 'peel-off' system on their parking slips where you can 'stick' the ticket to your window. Instead, these tickets have to be lain flat on the dashboard, (causing situations like the one I will outline below). I read the slip of paper within the plastic wallet and I gleaned the following facts :

Issuing officer's number : 50 (*not his age, he was at least double that*)

The notice number : NC14056890 (*This must be the number of tickets issued by this attendant so far that day given the circumstances of this one*)

Type : 2 (*Your ticket tells me that there are two types (type 1 and type 2) it does not however tell me what the difference between the two is – which would be helpful*)

Date : **/09/2007 (*One of the only things on this slip of paper that I can deem factual, though given the amount of fiction on the rest of the slip, I even begin to doubt that this was indeed the date*)

Time (*and this is important, I hope you are paying attention*) : 18:19 (*That's 6:19pm in old money*) – a time which you will notice is between the 17:22 when I bought the ticket and the 19:28 when the ticket expired.

Parking Place : Dean Street Multi (*True – well done to the parking attendant for knowing where he works*)

Bay Number : na (*Not sure if this is indeed the bay number – just as an aside, when I saw the ticket my immediate reaction was that we'd parked in one of those where you need a 'Willy Wonka' style gold ticket – with the 'Newcastle Gold Parking Club' sign behind it. But there was no such sign and as I said before, the bay was 1 (ONE) away from the office of the issuing officer (50)*)

Reg number : **** *** (*Not the most difficult eye test the older gentleman in the parking attendants outfit has ever had to complete*)

Make and Model : Peugeot 206 (*A car owned by someone trying to get out of paying a pound to park for 2 hours?*)

Colour : Grey (*the same as the attendants hair*)

Excise Lic. No : 1774375 (*Is this how much money you have made out of falsely claimed parking fine money?*)

Expiry date: 31/01/20** (*Is this the expiry date of the attendant?*)

Place of Lic. Issue : (*this bit was blank – much like the attendants expression when I questioned him about the issue of said ticket*)

"an authorised officer of the council noticed that the driver had contravened the above order by: A valid ticket was not displayed." (*Not only is the English in this sentence appalling, I doubt that the authorised officer 'noticed' anything, being as he was, heavily under the influence of Horlicks*)

We are expected to pay £60 – or £30 if paid within 7 days of issue (please note this timescale in reference to the latter part of the letter). £30 isn't exactly going to bankrupt me (though the amount you charge in tax on fuel might) and so if in the wrong, would happily pay this charge. However, when taking the excess ticket, along with the parking ticket I had obtained from the machine and displayed on the dashboard of the car to the attendants office (at which point I had to knock on the door as the attendant was not in his little room with the TV monitor, radio and various reading paraphernalia the council so keenly provide for him. He was in the back, with the blinds drawn – one of the hanging slats was slightly out of kilter with the rest which enabled me to see a kettle, a fridge and a family size jar of Horlicks in the room but not the attendant – who was probably trying to locate the door by feeling around the walls) and showing them to the attendant, he responded with a series of grunts through the circular voice hole in the centre of the glass partition. I remonstrated politely with the aged gentleman who seemed not to understand the reason for my frustration and again grunted something about it being in the system and to contact the address on the ticket. He intimated that there was no ticket on the dashboard – maybe I should have left it in-situ and brought him to see it and realising his error, withdrawing the notice. I, however, had it in my hand to show him – this evidently did not prove to be enough evidence and he stood his ground, albeit rather shakily and with the assistance of the back of a nearby chair.

I have sent photocopies of both the ticket I purchased to permit me to use your car park legally, and the parking ticket we were issued with not-so-legally, mainly because (if your office is staffed with similar people to those you use in your car parks) I expect you'll either lose this letter, not be able to see it being displayed correctly or lose my evidence of parking legally. If your attendant is unable to see the tickets displayed on the dashboard, I suggest you employ someone who can, introduce 'sticky ticket' technology or maybe continue to employ this person as I'm sure most of the other patrons who have also displayed a valid ticket and received an unlawful fine cannot be bothered to write in and complain, thus increasing the amount of money the council can spend on bedtime drinks for their staff.

I would ask you to rescind this ticket with an apology for the frankly abysmal service offered by your car park staff within 7 days or, using your own timescales, I will go straight to the Local Government Ombudsman, copying in Ian Humphries (Corporate complaints officer), the head of democratic services, my local councillor, MP and if necessary, my solicitor. I think it would be worth advising all of these people of the abject ineptitude of their car park staff – and in lieu of a withdrawal, the tardy response period of the office staff.

I await your response (within 7 days, let's see if you can keep to your own timescales).

P.S. I'm sure the parking attendant is a very nice man outside of work and understand he is only doing his job (albeit sleepily).

Kind Regards,

Peter Nuttall

abject ineptitude of our car parking staff. You are of course perfectly entitled to do so if that is what you feel is required.

That aside, given that this is the first such instance I am prepared to waive the charge and payment is excused. I may not however be able to take a similar view should there be any future recurrence.

Yours faithfully

Parking Team Manager

OLD ORLEANS

iNTERTAIN Ltd
Rowley House
Complaints Department
South Herts Office Campus
Elstree Way
Borehamwood
Herts, WD6 1JH

Dear Mr Orleans,

I've been dining in your Old Orleans restaurant since 1997 (with breaks to go to work and the shops etc.). I would sip fine cocktails and enjoy alligator and chips among other wonderful taste-bud tingling fare. I have bad news however; whenever I become particularly fond of something, it disappears. I got hooked on wispas then they withdrew them from sale. I couldn't get enough Kellogg's 'Chocolate Wheats' and the very next day, they stopped manufacturing them. It was inevitable then, that when I visited the fine City of York I found your restaurant closed down. I went to the one in Newcastle instead – only for it to close down too. Things don't look great for your Sunderland branch if I'm honest.

This isn't the reason for my complaint however. My tale begins when I signed up for your e-mail newsletter. It informs me every month that if I print a voucher off your website, it will entitle me to '2 meals for the price of 1'. This is marvellous as it enables me to cram twice as much Creole into my mouth as I would normally be able to (this is particularly important as soon, my nearest restaurant will be in Birmingham). It's the terms and conditions of use that baffle me. I work in marketing and so understand the huge importance of data capture (you ask me to fill in my name, date of birth and e-mail address as my age dictates whether you should put a picture of a coconut shrimp at the top of your e-shot, or a slightly exhausted looking crocodile). My bafflement is caused by your assertion that I cannot use the voucher unless I have 'pre-booked' a table.

No offence but whenever I go to your Sunderland restaurant, it's hardly standing room only. What possible benefit is it to you if I pre-book a table? You already know how many people are using vouchers, because you have to hand it in. What if I book a table, don't turn up and someone turns up on a whim and is turned away because the only table left is the one I'm not going to use?

Two weeks ago I was out and about and decided to visit your restaurant – I happened to have a voucher on me for emergencies. I turned up at 12pm just as the doors were being unlocked and walked in. I ordered my food and then informed the manageress (I assume she was the manageress as she was dressed differently to the rest of the staff (actually, there was also a bloke at the bar dressed as a jester so he was either the manager or was on the first leg of a stag do)) that I had a voucher but was unable to pre-book a table as the restaurant had only just opened. She shot me a look which suggested I'd just requested one of her own kidneys for dinner and said "Hmph! This time only but don't let it happen again". At this assertion, I suggested that I go out into the car park and ring her from my mobile in order to book a table then re-enter the building, thus activating the 'pre-book' clause of the voucher. She seemed non-plussed by this and wandered off.

The following week, I rang your restaurant at 12pm to pre-book a table and the gentleman who answered the phone seemed completely confused about why I was calling ahead. Mainly I suppose because when I turned up at 12:30, there were only 8 people in the entire building and four of those were staff. He asked 'is it for a birthday'? A strange question to which I informed him I was only booking a table because my voucher told me to. Could you please please please tell me why you have to pre-book to validate the voucher?? Surely someone real, standing in front of you with their voucher is worth more than a promise? Surely someone willing to pay full price because they have no idea you run a voucher on your website is more important than a promise? Does the telephone number I have to ring to book the table cost me the same as a plate of fajitas and this is how you recoup your costs? Please help me. How would you feel if you'd bought a puzzle book and it had no answers in the back?

Yours Confused,

Peter Nuttall

Mr. Nuttall

Monday 4th April 2011

Dear Mr. Nuttall

Re: Your visit to Old Orleans in Sunderland

Thank you for your letter dated 29th March concerning your recent visit to our Old Orleans restaurant in Sunderland. Your feedback is greatly appreciated as it helps us maintain the high standards set throughout our company.

The 'pre-book your table' clause, for the voucher offer is in place to ensure the correct staffing levels are maintained during the offer period. As you can imagine this is a very popular offer where we get between 350-500 bookings per week, lots of which are large parties celebrating for various reasons. This also helps us to evenly space the bookings so that there is no wait for service and ensures that customers are able to be seated rather than turned away as we have no room for them, which would happen at certain times if we didn't insist that tables are pre-booked.

I have revisited staff training regarding the booking procedure for the vouchers, so to ensure a consistent message to all customers wishing to use the offer.

Once again thank you for your feedback, we look forward to seeing you again soon enjoying the Old Orleans cuisine.

Yours sincerely

Gilbert Warburton
General Manager
Old Orleans Sunderland

INTERTAIN Limited, 3rd Floor, Rowley House, South Hams Office Campus, Elstree Way, Borehamwood, Herts, WD6 1HH
Tel 020 8327 2540, Fax 020 8327 2541
Registered Office as above. Registered number: 6996339 England

BRITVIC

Britvic Consumer Care,
PO Box 15503,
Shirley,
Solihull,
B90 9GG

Dear Mr. Pepsi,

Now I like to think of myself as a *real* man. I don't mean in the sense that I have all the necessary equipment so to prove the fact anatomically, nor do I mean in the metaphysical sense (or even a 'real man' which involves wiggling two fingers either side of my head). No, what I mean is that I don't need to have a big car to reflect/compensate for the size of certain parts of me or act aggressively towards other members of my community to 'assert' my masculinity. I can be commanding and confident when needs be, I open doors for members of the fairer sex and I am equally comfortable expressing my emotions openly; in cinemas for example (normally as I hand over a crisp twenty pound note for two and half bits of popcorn and some brown water masquerading as 'Cola' where even the water in it has been watered down) and accepting that I may only be able to drink three pints of beer before I need a sit down without having to have a chugging contest with two people whose alcohol stream has around 2% blood in it and think it's somehow a way of deciding who is more of a man than the other.

It has left me with somewhat of a dilemma though – which of your sugar-free beverages to choose! The alpha male, who is more at home in the gardening department of Asda than the fizzy drinks aisle, would be more prone to choosing Pepsi Max – allowing him to demonstrate everything his testosterone levels have rendered him capable of. Lifting a trolley full of frozen chickens with one hand while wiping away the froth from his bushy moustache from his third can of 'Max' with the other, that kind of thing. He would not, however, be happy doing a hundred squat thrusts with a small child on his back in front of some hopelessly impressed scantily clad women if afterwards he had to grab a can of chilled 'Diet Pepsi', take a swig and then drag it across his sweaty forehead whilst gazing ruggedly into the middle distance.

Inversely, I get the feeling that there are few slimming conscious women who would purchase a drink without the word 'diet' on the front. I work with a woman who really believes that she can have a house special kebab with garlic and chilli sauce, followed by a tub of Haagen Dasz as long as she has a diet pepsi to accompany the meal. She can't understand why she keeps putting on weight! Also, could you have a word with your friends at *coca cola* about their 'Diet Coke break' advert. The bloke in it is about as attractive as an ingrown toe nail that's got all infected. It's just not realistic. I think they're copying off you too with their 'coke zero' and 'diet coke' brands which are one in the same thing surely? One has no sugar in it and the other has erm... no sugar in it!

Anyway, I digress; You have put me in a virtually untenable situation – do I choose 'Pepsi Max', and give in to the side of me that wants to own a big pair of headphones and a 45 inch HD ready multi-function TV or do I choose 'Diet Pepsi' and allow that side of me that wants to burst into tears at the merest hint of an injured puppy to surface. I like to keep the balance between to two, androgynous harmony if you will; however you don't sell a drink that allows me to maintain this balance.

Please tell me the difference between your drinks so I can make an informed choice!

Yours Confusedly,

Peter Nuttall

Mr Peter Nuttall

Reference Number
110330-000015

30/3/2011

Dear Mr Nuttall,

Thank you for your letter.

Pepsi Max and Diet Pepsi basically have the same ingredients. The difference is the levels of each ingredient, which give the products their different flavours.

Britvic will supply its trade customers with the information necessary to assist them to comply with their legal obligations and to demonstrate due diligence with regard to compliance.

We are aware of and comply with our statutory and common law obligations to our customers and consumers, and we support industry schemes for disclosure of ingredients to which consumers may have an intolerance.

However, we believe that the certain information is of a commercially sensitive and competitive nature which, if divulged, could affect our ability to compete freely and fairly with our competitors. This includes details of our raw material suppliers and he origin of raw materials used as well as the specific formula and recipe information other than ingredients lists.

However, in order to make things clearer, all ingredients on all food and drink products have to be listed in order of quantity from highest to lowest. So you will notice that the order of ingredients on Diet Pepsi and Pepsi Max are different.

Yours sincerely,

• ROBINSONS • TANGO • PEPSI • BRITVIC • J₂O/JUICES • 7UP • FRUIT SHOOT • ORANGINA • MR. • J₂J • GATORADE • PURDEY'S •

PEPSICO (WALKERS)

PepsiCo International Ltd,
FAO Walkers Crisps People
63 Kew Road,
Richmond,
Surrey,
TW9 2QL

Dear Sir,

You may think that my letter is a little belated, coming as it has at least 15 years after your transgression but it has taken me that long to readjust to society since you smashed all traces of British tradition and started to put salt and vinegar crisps in green bags. I wasn't so bothered about Ready Salted being in red bags, because they are a 'Reddy' colour and I quite liked that, but when I first opened one of your blue bags only to be met with the stench of a tramp's feet – it took me several years of vacuous musings before gathering my scattered emotions into some semblance of that which you would expect of a person who is at peace with themselves.

I experienced my first crisp related trauma when I opened a packet of Smith's Ready Salted only to realise after much frantic crisp jostling, that there was no little blue bag included containing the statutory 4 grains of salt. This forced me to raid the yellow 'Grit' bin at the end of my street, then spend many weeks in a coma in my local hospital. The next trial involved an 'over-flavoured' packet of Pickled Onion *Monster Munch* in which I almost lost a kidney followed by a poignant moment when I lifted a scampi and lemon *Nik-Nak* out of its bag to find it resembled an ex-girlfriend's face. I also took umbrage to the fact that there are less crisps in a 'big eat' bag of crisps than there is in a normal bag. Then came what I considered to be the faux-pas to end all faux-pas (sorry, not sure what the plural is there), when someone thought it would be a good idea to combine chocolate and crisps. They didn't do what I thought may have worked, which was putting the crisp inside a lump of chocolate – they 'flavoured' the crisp with cocoa or something similar. Correct me if I'm wrong, but isn't that a bit like crossing the streams in Ghostbusters?

The final thing to tip my mind over the rock face of madness was the 'dirty feet' incident described at the top of my letter. What is going on? Salt and Vinegar (which in real life are white and brown/transparent respectively) always come in a blue bag! Don't ask me why – they just do. It's like why does the sun come up? It just does! Cheese and Onion (which in real life can both have green bits on them) come in a green bag! Again, it's like why is a cloud fluffy? It just is! It led me to organise a self-help therapy group at my local community centre in which we bought paper bags, painted them blue and green and then placed a correct flavour crisp into each. This stabilised my mind enough to form a group called "The **C**ampaign for the **R**e-alignment **I**n the **S**hade of **P**otato **S**nacks" or C.R.I.S.P.S. for short. Reminding ourselves day after day of the dismay that you have inflicted on our lives by your frolicsome re-colouration of your bags soon led to this organisation disbanding.

I don't think you understand! At least 3 other people have posted stuff on the internet about it and I'm sure I saw a petition somewhere (which actually made me realise there might be more important things going on in the world for a moment) asking you to change the colours back. You could even do a swanky advertising campaign featuring the ever-so-nice Gary 'slightly creepy' Lineker stealing crisps off people in another hilarious scenario. I managed to cope with *Jif* changing its name to *Cif*, I managed to remain in control of my faculties while *Opal Fruits* had their identity stripped and although I know you're not responsible for these, I still feel a little bit angry at you because they changed the name of *Marathon* to *Snickers*. I'm sure you can appreciate that change isn't always for the better unless you really have to break into a twenty pound note.

Please let me know what you're proposing to do about this diabolical sham!

Yours,

Peter Nuttall

P.S. I have also recently noticed that Curlie-Wurlies aren't as big as they used to be – but maybe it's just that my expectations are higher than when I was a child? Please let me know your thoughts.

Customer Services
Freephone UK: 0800 274 777
Freephone EIRE: 1800 509 408
Fax: 0116 234 8691

000302591A

12 April 2011

Mr Peter Nuttall

Dear Mr Nuttall

Thank you very much for your recent letter.

The principal reason for our Cheese & Onion packets being blue and our Salt & Vinegar being green is quite simply that they have always been that colour. We have found that our customers relate easily to these distinctive colours.

We realise other crisp manufacturers use the pack colours the other way round but we feel that if we changed our colours now it would be totally confusing to many people.

In regards to the Salt & Shake, the salt sachets are inserted into the packets in an automated process and it would appear that a temporary machine fault has occurred and I am sorry that you no salt sachets in your packets.

On all of our products we ask for consumers to send the packaging and contents to us if they have reason for complaint. We are then able to identify, from the codes on the packaging, the factory and production line of manufacture. This information enables the relevant factory to identify and correct any fault that may have occurred.

Unfortunately, as the packaging and contents were not sent to us, we are unable to fully investigate the complaint for you.

If you do have any more faulty packets please send to the freepost address below:

Walkers Snacks Limited
Customer Services Department
FREEPOST LE4 918
Leicester
LE4 5ZY

We really appreciate hearing from our consumers who take the trouble to let

Walkers Snack Foods Ltd, PO Box 23, Leicester, LE4 5CD.
Registered Office: New Arlington Business Park, Theale, RG7 4SA. Registered No. 733102.

us know their preferences regarding our products.   We are very sorry to hear that you did not like Walkers Chilli & Chocolate flavour crisps.   We are always very happy to receive consumer feedback and please be assured that I have forwarded your comments on to our Marketing Team for their attention.

Once again, thank you for taking the time and trouble to contact us, it is very much appreciated.   If you do have any more queries, please do not hesitate to contact me again.

Yours sincerely

Mandeep Riyat
Mandeep Riyat
Customer Services

SUNDERLAND CITY COUNCIL

From: Peter Nuttall
Sent: 19 October 2008 11:25
To: customer.services@sunderland.gov.uk
Subject: Complaint

Dear Sir,

I must firstly apologise if my spelling is not up to scratch in this complaint letter. You see, I have a condition known as 'delayed shock syndrome' which makes me react to scares and frights a while after receiving the initial surprise. As this letter wears on, you will see the reasons behind my spastic and convulsive behaviour in places such as Starbucks, where all is tranquil and calm.

It is ironic that my eyesight at this moment is rather foggy, as the reason for it being so is in fact… Fog. It is not foggy in my office where I type you understand, that would be silly, it's far too warm and the relative humidity has not yet reached 100%. No, I am talking of Sea fog. You see, because the sea is full of salt, and the ocean spray throws thousands of tiny particles of salt up into the atmosphere around which atmospheric water can condense, there has been a need for a large trumpet by the sea to entertain sailors who's radios have broken and to guide mariners safely away from rocks because the lighthouse can't be bothered to change their light bulb from a 40 to a 60.

Imagine for a second that you are tootling along merrily in your little tug boat, catching crabs with your wife when all of a sudden a blanket of fog descends upon your little ship. What do you do? You don't want to crash into a rock! You go full steam ahead to the shore where you can moor up your tug and take your crabs home to be treated. Your passage to shore of course is aided by an ear-splitting trumpet every few seconds which is cleverly coded so you know to turn left at that jaggy rock and right at the cliff! Could it be that people think the trumpety blast is there to frighten the fog that it may disperse? It only seems to have one function to me – and that is to emulate a Tesco delivery van in waking me up at all hours of the morning!!

I'm not up on modern technology but has it occurred to anyone to fit a boat with a rock seeking device? Turn it on, and use the Sat-Nav system to guide you to your destination. Although if it's anything like the one I got at Halfords for £49.99 on Saturday, it will guide you to the nearest Halfords, whatever you type in! Gone are the days when the mermaids known to the Greeks as 'Sirens', lured sailors to their deaths. These days of course, when the Sirens sing their haunting song from the shore, people just think the cliff is having a fire drill so they phone the fire brigade who promptly deal with the situation. Also, when mermaids leave the sea, their tails turn into legs, so they're all working in *Subway* now (it sounds like submarine and reminds them of home).

It will not surprise you to learn that I live in close proximity to the sea. When I first moved there I imagined the splendour of waking up in the summer, the sun bleaching my window, the seagulls barking their croaky song and the haunting melodies tinkling spookily out of a disused amusement arcade down the road. Instead, I get blasted awake every four seconds depending on the density of the fog (9 seconds = 9 knots of visibility). There are 3 near me and when they all go off at different times, not only do the sailors think there must be 1000 knots of visibility (as they form a continuous noise for 1000 seconds – please, keep up), but when they do fall out of kilter with each other I can only get 4 nano-seconds of sleep every 1000 seconds.
I say turn off the fog horns!! Teach those salty sea dogs a lesson. Avast ye land lubbers, me harties, make them walk the plank for their troubles. Let them crash into rocks, it's their fault for being on a boat in the first place in hazardous conditions. You could also turn off the light houses which I'm sure are wired into my electrical mains as my electricity bill seems far higher than anyone else in my street! The amount of light houses on my bit of coast is the equivalent of the number of hundreds and thousands on a Greggs' sprinkly do-nut!

If we turn off these horns it will also stop the people who operate the noisy trumpets from making the same joke over and over – "It's foggy, shall we give the sailor's the horn?" It's not funny! Stop it!

I await your response.

Kind Regards,

Peter Nuttall

From: *Colin Clark [mailto:Colin.Clark@sunderland.gov.uk]*
Sent: *23 October 2008 14:30*
To: *nutfox@blueyonder.co.uk*
Cc: *Margaret Douglas; Linda Watmore; Neil Mearns*
Subject: *Complaint*

Mr Nuttall

Thank you for your e mail of the 16th of October 2008 in which you raise concerns regarding the operation of the fog horn at Roker.

The Port of Sunderland, as Local Lighthouse Authority, has a statutory responsibility under Merchant Shipping Acts to provide, maintain and test fog signalling apparatus. This is required as an aid to navigation for shipping and small craft during periods of reduced visibility. Whenever foggy conditions occur, the port control is required to activate the Roker Pier fog signal, together with that on the Old North Pier (when poor visibility prevails within the inner harbour). As these signals must comply with prescribed criteria, it is not possible to reduce the sound level. Visibility is closely monitored to ensure that signals are switched off once it improves to an acceptable level.

I am sorry that the signals give you such cause for concern, but hope that you are able to appreciate that they are a statutory requirement. I hope this response is satisfactory. If however, you feel that it has not addressed your concerns, then you can ask for your complaint to be dealt with at Stage 2 of the council's customer services procedure. If you wish to do this please write to the Complaints Co-ordinator, Development and Regeneration, PO Box 102, Civic Centre, Sunderland, SR2 7DN.

Regards,

Colin Clark

TESCO 1

From: Peter Nuttall
Sent: 15 August 2008 13:40
To: customer.service@tesco.co.uk
Subject: Crack of dawn deliveries

Dear Sir,

I wish to draw your attention away from the Internet (which you are no doubt casually perusing while wondering which DVD you are going to watch when you get in) and towards an on-going incidence of what I like to refer to as 'that bloody Tesco van again' or to be more specific, the vehicle that performs deliveries for your Tesco Extra Express Stores.

The store I refer to is situated in Main Street, Dickens Heath, Solihull. I would look up the post-code but I am sure you are probably too busy scratching yourself while reading this and thinking about what flavour muffins are your favourite rather than listen to the concerns of one of your 'valued' customers.

Every morning, and I exclude Sundays when God (who features strongly in my swear-word laden appraisal of these incidents to my partner every morning) declared that everyone should be 'resting', we are rudely awakened by your delivery vehicles. This can start from anything as early as 6am when the dulcet rattle of cages being delicately tugged from the back of your 6 tonne articulated lorries floats majestically over the rooftops and directly into my ears. This rattling brings back a bad memory of mine involving a banana skin and a large Xylophone.

Whilst we appreciate deliveries must be made, we also appreciate your fresh food, dedication to satisfying your customers and those *oh-so-valuable* Tesco Club Card points (incidentally I have collected 60,000 and now have enough for a small key-ring). We feel not only constantly tired but surprised at the amount of noise your drivers seem able to make with a packet of *snack-a-jacks*.

I would suggest that these deliveries could be made either more quietly or at a later more sociable time; around 3pm perhaps? Even if some consideration could be made on weekends, when I'm sure you would appreciate, people can be a little worse for wear. The noise disturbs not only me but also my elderly grandmother who lives next door (granted, she has been disturbed since the Second World War).

If you have read this far, and haven't fallen asleep into your large mug of Tesco 'Finest', I would be eminently grateful if you could consider providing the delivery crews with furry slippers with sponge soles, (I would recommend George at ASDA '£3.99 for size 8') this could be funded by the removal of Mr Terry Wogan from voicing your adverts (in my opinion this is just fuelling his well-known vices).

Every little helps !

Yours Sincerely,

Peter Nuttall

From: Tesco Customer Service customer.service@tesco.co.uk
To: Peter Nuttall
Subject: TES2846144

Thank you for your email.

I was sorry to learn of the problems that you have encountered with regard to store deliveries in your area and would like to apologise for the upset caused.

I am looking into this matter and as soon as I have any further information, I will contact you again.

Thank you for your patience.

If you have any further queries please do not hesitate to contact us at customer.service@tesco.co.uk quoting TES2846144.

Kind Regards

Suzi Harris
Tesco Customer Service

TESCO 2

From: Peter Nuttall
Sent: 19 August 2008 12:21
To: customer.service@tesco.co.uk
Subject: Re: TES2359144X

Dear Ms Harris,

Thank you for your prompt reply – though when the e-mail arrived it did make my computer ping rather loudly, which brought about an episode not dissimilar to the night terrors I experience when I hear your vans outside my house. Having calmed down sufficiently, I notice that you work for the customer service division, rather than the distribution department. It would be helpful if you forward the e-mail on to the 'cage noise reduction manager' and hopefully I will receive a response that actually deals with the issue rather than tells me that I am 'upset' by what has happened. I can tell you that the noise doesn't cause me 'upset' it causes me deafness, lack of sleep, mild tantrums and marital difficulties.

I have also recently noticed that when I hear certain songs, I tend to start clawing at my ears and shouting 'Bloody Tesco' at the top of my voice. The songs in question include 'She bangs' by Ricky Martin, 'Club (card) Tropicana' by Wham (which is incidentally the noise made when the cages are shoved back into place) and 'Signed, Sealed, Delivered' by Stevie Wonder, to which now I can only hear '*Whined, squealed*, delivered'. I await your reply with interest; you may wish to send it at about 6am, as I will no doubt be awake anyway while the Uncle Ben, Danone and Heinz of this world are being sonorously tugged from their metal hauliers but a few inches from my bedroom window.

It may please you to know that this episode *has* helped to protect the environment however as I no longer have use for your plastic bags (which are made of the thinnest plastic your scientists could create), as I am now using the bags under my eyes to carry my weeklies in.

Yours Sincerely,

Peter Nuttall

From: *Tesco Customer Service* *customer.service@tesco.co.uk*
To: *Peter Nuttall*
Subject: *TES2846144*

Thank you for your email.

I have been asked to inform you to speak with the store manager regarding this
Issue. If this proves unsuccessful you should then raise the issue of noise with
your local councils Environmental Health Department.

I hope this information helps you.

Thank you for bringing this matter to our attention.

If you have any further queries please do not hesitate to contact us at
customer.service@tesco.co.uk quoting TES2846144

Kind Regards

Suzi Harris
Tesco Customer Service

Conclusion

Whether you've just bought an eight hundred pound mobile phone that can make your tea and cut your toenails, or a loaf of bread from the corner shop there will be something in consumer law that protects you. Obviously, not all vendors are as aware of the law as they could be hence the existence of BBC's Watchdog and Trading Standards. Everybody makes mistakes and every company is going to make mistakes. You should not judge a company on the mistakes it makes but on the way they correct them. If the bread you bought was mouldy, it's quite reasonable to expect the shop to exchange it for you with a smile. It is not reasonable to expect them to give you a ten minute 'supermarket sweep' where you keep what you can pile in your trolley, as compensation.

A lot of the customers I've dealt with in the past have made unrealistic demands; deciding which I could pacify with a fifty pound gratuity and which would only drop legal proceedings if I agreed to pay for their entire upstairs to be re-carpeted was the challenge. Where there's a grey area in the law, there's room for negotiation. Where there's blame on both sides, there's a chance that were the client to take the case down the legal route, they'd end up winning compensation of a few thousand pounds. One customer in particular had her new kitchen installation delayed by seven days. She told the court that in each of those seven days she and her family had to eat out, such was the lack of access to cooking appliances. On the first night she went to the local chip shop which cost her twelve pounds. On the second night, and each successive night she dined out at a five star restaurant, costing her sixty pounds. Her claim was for over four hundred pounds. The judge awarded her eighty four pounds, stating that she could have had a take away meal on each of the nights her kitchen was out of action. The lesson here I suppose is to give the complaint handler every reason to want to help you. I probably would have given the customer the four hundred pounds she'd asked for had the relationship not started with a letter littered with threats and capital letters.

When it comes to compensation, a company cannot put a price on stress but the cost of a plumber coming out to fix the leak caused by the bathroom fitter putting his foot through the ceiling is quantifiable. Those who'd thrown their old bed away awaiting the delivery of the new one, only to find it didn't arrive on the day it was due, would have a case for recompense. The people delivering the bed are not responsible for the fact the customer has thrown their own bed out and they now have nowhere to sleep but if the customer has to take another day's holiday from work to wait in for the delivery, then that would be considered for a goodwill gesture. In one case, a customer was told his bookcase would be delivered before twelve o'clock. It turned up at one o'clock and she missed the afternoon session at the bingo. I felt it unrealistic to meet her demands of refunding the cost of the bookcase in lieu of the fact she could have won three hundred pounds in the *Mecca* super jackpot.

In regards to the letters I sent while writing this book, I have only included the ones I received replies to. I didn't receive replies from the various public houses I wrote to, meaning they either don't care about their customers or they don't have a dedicated person responsible for customer service; probably the latter. Large retailers will have a team of people dedicated to after sales service; this doesn't necessarily mean they're bad at what they do and need a team to 'mop up' the service carnage. Although, in the case of the bigger corporations such as *Cineworld*, I can only assume that the letters I sent were 'lost' in the system or passed to someone who was having a bad day. I did eventually receive a response to my third letter. My letter to '*Louis Tussaud*' which is still unanswered serves as a lesson that you need to make sure you're contacting the correct people. The waxwork museum at the time was owned by *Leisure Parcs Ltd*, and so the letter should have been copied to them and not just sent to the Waxwork museum in Blackpool. The letter I wrote to 'Advantage Loans' did just that. I advised them at the bottom of the letter that I was contacting the company that owned them, just to ensure they didn't 'lose' my letter in the bin. I was reimbursed with my fee within five days. This letter isn't included in this book because their response came in the form of a phone call; it is however available to read on www.iwanttocomplain.net, as are the letters I didn't receive replies to.

Tesco were professional in the face of a complaint they really couldn't do much about and ASDA replied within five working days to offer apologies and gift cards for both of my complaints. Local Government departments were very quick and helpful too, cancelling a parking ticket and explaining why the fog horns are really necessary. If a company accepts complaints via e-mail then this seems the best way to communicate. *Itiswhatitis.co.uk* responded within 24 hours and offered a refund or a goodwill gesture. *Virgin Media* responded quickly and rectified the issue to my satisfaction; they are players in a very competitive market so it is imperative that they put customer satisfaction high on their list of priorities. I received good humoured replies to some of the more frivolous complaints. *Nestlé* certainly entered into the spirit of what I was hoping to achieve by sending me four 'old style' Smarties tubes. Golden Wonder and Cadbury also proved that the slogan they print on their confectionary packets about welcoming customer feedback is true. *Pepsico*, being a huge corporation, were particularly difficult to contact. They do welcome e-mails but I found it difficult to find an address to write to and more importantly, the name of the person responsible for managing their customer service team; it is worth the effort in the long run however.

Although the people who take your money should look after you, it is important to understand the challenges faced by those companies in providing you with excellent service. Customer service is a stressful job which in turn leads to high staff turnover. This means there will be a lack of consistency in the level of the experience of their staff and a very different response to the same complaint from advisor to advisor. Because staff retention can be difficult and therefore the majority are inexperienced, the purported swiftness in dealing with complaints suffers. If, as a consumer, we can help these people enjoy their jobs then they'll stay longer, be more consistent, build better client relationships, be more efficient and you'll get a better outcome than if you swore at them in red pen.

P.S. If you have any complaints about this book, direct them via the website and please make them amusing.